Understanding the Emotional Needs of Children in the Early Years

This accessible book focuses on the emotional needs, experiences and development of young children, exploring the role of the practitioner in ensuring that each and every child feels loved, supported and safe; able to develop secure attachments and flourish in the first five years and beyond.

Drawing upon neuro-scientific research and referencing key theories relating to attachment, and health and wellbeing, the book examines the responsibilities of the early years practitioner in supporting children to reach their full potential. The response of the adult to the emotional needs of individual children is analysed in detail, and the impacts of various experiences, cultures and contexts on a child's emotional wellbeing are considered. With topics including safeguarding, communication, the physical environment, neurological development and Attachment Theory, readers will:

- learn how to respond appropriately to individual children

- extend their role as a Key Person and their position in a multi-professional team

- increase their understanding of the interaction between home and childcare settings

- reflect on the importance of in-depth observation, the environment and quality of care provided in their settings.

Supported by rich case studies, provocations and examples of good practice to encourage reflection and improve future practice, *Understanding the Emotional Needs of Children in the Early Years* is an engaging and comprehensive guide for all early years practitioners, early years students and professionals including paediatric nurses, health visitors and social workers.

Tricia Johnson is former Senior Lecturer and subject specialist for the FdA Early Years and BA Practice Development (Early Years) at Buckinghamshire New University, UK.

Understanding the Emotional Needs of Children in the Early Years

Tricia Johnson

Routledge
Taylor & Francis Group

LONDON AND NEW YORK

First published 2018
by Routledge
2 Park Square, Milton Park, Abingdon, Oxon OX14 4RN

and by Routledge
711 Third Avenue, New York, NY 10017

Routledge is an imprint of the Taylor & Francis Group, an informa business

British Library Cataloguing in Publication Data
A catalogue record for this book is available from the British Library

Library of Congress Cataloging in Publication Data
Names: Johnson, Tricia, 1946- author.
Title: Understanding the emotional needs of children in the early years /
    Tricia Johnson.
Description: Abingdon, Oxon ; New York, NY : Routledge, 2018. |
    Includes bibliographical references and index.
Identifiers: LCCN 2017060477 (print) | LCCN 2018012670 (ebook) |
    ISBN 9781138228849 (hbk) | ISBN 9781138228856 (pbk) | ISBN
    9781315391502 (ebk)
Subjects: LCSH: Early childhood education—Psychological aspects. |
    Emotions in children.
Classification: LCC LB1139.23 (ebook) | LCC LB1139.23 .J67 2018 (print) |
    DDC 372.21—dc23
LC record available at https://lccn.loc.gov/2017060477

ISBN: 978-1-138-22884-9 (hbk)
ISBN: 978-1-138-22885-6 (pbk)
ISBN: 978-1-315-39150-2 (ebk)

Typeset in Melior
by Swales & Willis Ltd, Exeter, Devon, UK

MIX
Paper from responsible sources
FSC
www.fsc.org FSC® C013056

Printed and bound in Great Britain by
TJ International Ltd, Padstow, Cornwall

Contents

About the author

Tricia Johnson is an Early Years' consultant with a broad range of experience, having worked as a lecturer and head of school for Early Years in Further Education and as a Senior Lecturer in Higher Education with the roles of course leader for the Sector Endorsed Foundation Degree and Pathway Leader for the BA (Hons) Practice Development (Early Years), both of which she helped to develop at Buckinghamshire New University. She is an experienced Early Years Practitioner having initially helped at her local preschool and then combined her nursing qualification with a lifelong ambition to work with children; she was employed by The Norland College for 14 years. During this time she worked in the Children's Hotel, a registered children's home, on night duty, as Deputy and then Manager caring for children aged from ten days to nine years. She also managed the Day Care unit for children aged from three months to three years of age. Tricia was a member of the Local Early Years Partnership, chairing the quality and training sub groups and was also involved in writing the guidance to accompany the National Standards for the Regulation of Day Care (2000). She is currently a committee member for the Sector Endorsed Foundation Degree Early Years Professional Association (SEFDEY), an advisory committee member for her local Pre-School and Froebel Travelling Tutor.

Acknowledgements

I would like to thank all members of my family, especially my husband, my friends and colleagues with whom I have had many discussions about the content and progression of this book. Thank you!

Introduction

Key themes within this book

This book has been written to help you:

- Gain a deeper understanding of the emotional needs of very young children and of how to respond appropriately to the children

- Increase your knowledge and understanding of the important phases of brain development

- Deepen your knowledge and understanding of the importance of secure attachment, and of separation anxiety and the effects of insecure attachment

- Fully understand the important role you have in the lives of the children in your care, particularly the Key Person Role, and their position in a multi-professional team

- Analyse and strengthen your Partnerships with Parents

- Increase your understanding of the impact of different cultures experienced by very young children such as home and childcare settings

- Reflect on the effects of your own childhood experiences when responding to young children

- Reflect on the importance of in-depth observation to ensure effective response to the emotional needs of young children

- Consider and reflect on the environment and quality of care provided in your settings

- Provide a calm, caring environment that responds to the emotional and individual learning needs of every child in your setting.

The reason for writing this book and the focus on the emotional needs of very young children rather than emotional development is very closely linked to personal experiences as a young child when in hospital, experiences as a Registered Nurse, as a Mother and as a Childcare Professional. Practical and theoretical experience was gained in Pre-schools, a Children's Home and Day Care as a manager and then in Further and Higher Education, as a Head of School and Senior Lecturer. It was during these experiences that I realised the emotional needs of babies and very young children were not always being met. This was partly because there was not a full understanding of their 'emotional needs', because the focus was placed on social and emotional development and behaviour management without identifying the cause of behaviours and a child feeling 'sad'. The full understanding of the need for a secure attachment to a significant person, usually the Mother, and for a secure base was not fully appreciated until evidence from neuroscientific research into the development of the brain which provided strong support to Bowlby's theory of attachment.

My inpatient experience occurred prior to the implementation of extended visiting hours for children's wards. The visiting hours were extended following the results of research, undertaken by Bowlby (1950s), Ainsworth and the Robertson (1960s), into attachment, separation and strange situations (see Chapter 2). There were also experiences and incidents encountered during nurse training when working on children's wards and being told, 'don't go in and pick the babies up for a cuddle, you will make them cry even more when you leave them again.' The very unwell babies were in cots, with very few toys near them and in rooms on their own. At this stage of my training, I had not heard of attachment theory but just knew that this situation was wrong. Many of the babies did not receive visitors either. This was for many reasons such as distance to be travelled and the cost of travel, young siblings at home and, very sadly, parents disinterested in the babies who did not want to visit. Where were the caring and the sensitive responses to these babies when separated from their Mothers or first carers? Caring, sensitive responses were evident during care and treatment routines and during their feeds. In hindsight this approach was possibly linked to the number of children in the ward, the length of time that was spent in hospital and the levels of staffing. It could also have been related to a lack of understanding of attachment theory. One member of staff was a qualified Nursery Nurse who was mostly tasked with feeding and changing the babies, not playing with them. The culture within hospitals has, in this respect, changed for the better, there are now much longer visiting hours and accommodation is available in hospitals or nearby so that parents or carers of very ill children can stay.

The memory of being left in hospital is still vivid. It was an austere, clinical, unfriendly place that smelt strongly of disinfectants and other chemicals. I was with strangers i.e. nurses and other medical staff I did not know, when admitted to hospital at the age of eight years for planned orthopaedic surgery. It was terrifying, despite two previous visits to the ward. The first thing that happened to all children who were admitted for planned procedures was that, once your parents had left, you were taken to have a bath. This felt very intrusive. All I could say was, 'but I have already had a bath this morning'. The response was, 'well you're having another one now'. There was no explanation that the bath and other pre-operative preparation were part of the procedures for all orthopaedic admissions. They were obviously carried out to help prevent new bacterial infections being introduced into the ward or, more importantly, the operating theatres. These procedures were even more terrifying than being left alone. The procedure was completed; the nurses walked away. There was little respect shown or any acknowledgement of emotional needs. When I cried, I was told off because I would upset the rest of the children. I was also told that I would not be moved to the main ward with all of the other children until I stopped crying. Thank goodness, I had a kind, caring but assertive Mother, who, on hearing my story confronted the Ward Sister. The result, I was moved to the main ward and was immediately much happier; we even enjoyed singing sessions each day – very uplifting.

On reflecting on my own experience and observing such unhappy babies in hospital, my thoughts moved to think about what caused these memories to be reignited in me? Initially, this was when working on the Children's ward and then when I watched two films linked to Bowlby and the Robertsons' research – 'John' about a young boy who spent three weeks in a children's home and 'A two-year-old goes to hospital.' The title of the second film is self-explanatory. These films were also shown at a seminar on attachment. The impact on all the delegates in the room was almost tangible; there were several who had been in hospital around the time the films were being made. These films are discussed in Chapter 2, where you are invited to analyse the films in relation to experiences children have today. There is no inference here that separation anxiety does not occur when children are in hospital, in Early Years Settings or in care now. We know that it does.

Everyone needs to feel responded to, respected, loved, accepted, safe and secure but particularly babies and very young children, as was identified through the research by Bowlby and more recently Holmes (2001) and Trevarthen (2004)

> There is in every child at every stage a new miracle of vigorous unfolding, which constitutes a new hope and a new responsibility for all.
>
> (Erikson in Garhart Mooney 2000 p. 37)

The aim of this book is to primarily encourage Early Years academics, practitioners, students and other professionals such as Paediatric Nurses, Health Visitors and Social Workers to research, to extend and to think in greater depth about emotional needs, primarily of babies and very young children from conception until the age of five years. It refers to and uses theories and concepts relating to the history of Early Years, the importance of Attachment Theory and the recent, relevant research findings of Neuroscience. The focus on the emotional needs of children is maintained and referred to throughout. Whilst the focus of this book is the emotional needs of babies and very young children the holistic development of children is always considered.

Topics for debate such as the need for a child to be 'school ready', the reasons for an overly 'risk averse culture', the value of outdoor play, and the changing requirements of the Early Years Foundation Stage (2017) have been included. There is some mention of International Early Years Curricula and International research into *teachers' experiences of closeness in the classroom in Canada*, (Quan-McGimpsey, Leon Kuczynski; Kathleen Brophy (2011) in Chapters 3, 4 and 5.

The most recent debate that is developing in England is around the recent publication by Ofsted titled 'Bold Beginnings (November 2017). The publication has not been received with the enthusiasm that was expected because it appears to ignore the advice of Early Years Professionals. The document makes recommendations for children's attainment by the time they move into the Reception Class. The main focus is on their levels of ability in reading, writing, and mathematics that relate to Key Stage 1 of the National Curriculum. Ofsted recognises that 'the Reception Year is unique', which it is.

> TACTYC also concurs that the Reception year is 'important' and therefore requires that teachers are well trained and supported in suitable curriculum strategies and pedagogies that are appropriate for the early years, which arguably extend beyond the Reception year, particularly for summer-born children.
>
> > Association for the Professional Development of Early
> > Years Educators (TACTYC) December 2017 p. 1)

This concern is supported in the response to the Ofsted report on Bold Beginnings in Nursery World by Kym Scott (8 December 2017)

> And no recommendations are made around the areas that have been highlighted as being the real building blocks of future learning – Physical Development, Communication and Language and Personal, Social and Emotional Development and around promoting the Characteristics of Effective Learning, all of which are shown by research to be key indicators of later achievement. We have a mental health crisis looming in our young people and this report is not only a missed opportunity to address this but in some ways risks contributing to it, by encouraging schools to put our youngest children under increasing pressure.
>
> > (Scott 2017)

The current Government is proposing to test children between the ages of four and five, another initiative that is opposed by Early Years Professionals who continue to advocate that children up to the age of six and beyond should be learning through play. It is suggested that you access the; Bold Beginnings Report, the full responses related to the quotes above and the Government Proposal for testing four to five-year-olds.

Play provision, as you know, should be related to each child's abilities and interests, having observed what a child can do and using this as the starting point before extending their play and learning. All play will encourage development of the fine and gross motor skills that will ultimately enable each child to hold a pencil correctly!! Play that is child led, indoors and outdoors, that encourages their imagination, allows a child to fantasise, to internalise and make sense of the world around them through role play, for example in the home corner.

Case study 1

An example of children leading their own play followed a move to a new purpose-built Early Years setting where the outdoor area had been planted with several small shrubs. A group of two and three-year-olds were playing outside, not long after they had moved in, when a child pulled one of the shrubs out of the ground. The child was joined by other children and gradually, all of the shrubs were removed. The children then found the buckets and spades and started to dig and explore the soil. The area was never replanted, it became the outdoor, natural digging area where, with time, they would find worms and minibeasts besides the actual soil, stones and roots from nearby trees. The staff did not stop this exploration, they supported it, having first thought, oh dear, what will management say!! The needs of the children came first, the event was easily explained, and exploration continued.

For over four hundred years the importance of play and responding to the individual emotional and learning needs of babies and very young children has been identified and documented by theorists and Early Years Pioneers such as: John Amos Comenius, Jean-Jacques Rousseau, Sigmund Freud, Friedrich Froebel, Susan Isaacs, Margaret Donaldson, John Bowlby, Mary Ainsworth, the Robertsons and more recently Daniel Stern, Tina Bruce, Peter Elfer, Howard Steele, Jeremy Holmes, Alison Gopnik et al., Colwyn Trevarthen and Sue Gerhardt.

Consider this quote by Comenius from between 1628 and 1632:

The proper education of the young does not consist in stuffing their heads with a mass of words, sentences, and ideas dragged together out of various authors, but in opening up their understanding to the outer world, so that a living stream may flow from their own minds, just as leaves, flowers, and fruit spring from the bud on a tree.

(http://www.froebelweb.org/web7005.html
accessed 13 December 2017)

How true is this today? How upsetting is it to know that theorists and pioneers who identified the thirst for learning, the importance of play, the desire to communicate and the need for a freedom to learn, providing the emotional needs of the child were being responded to, are still not being listened to and heard?

You are reminded throughout the book about the impact of feeling emotionally insecure, lonely and unloved on the ability to learn and develop. The response of the adult to the needs of very young children is explored and analysed in detail, especially the way that the adult speaks to a baby or young child. What affects the responses of the adult? Have these responses been influenced by nature, our social cultures, our widest family cultures, immediate family culture and our experiences when we were young children ourselves? The term 'nuclear family' has purposely not been used here because, as you know, there are many different family structures in our society today which include the family comprising two generations of parents and children (nuclear family), single parent families and the different forms of extended family.

When a Key Person is asked why a child is so unhappy, how often do we still hear?

'Oh, he or she is so clingy, I can't move away from them. How can I care for the other key children and complete my other duties?'

Or,

'Oh, he is just having a bad day'.

If these situations are managed carefully and the baby or young child is provided with the love and comfort he or she is seeking at that time, the Key Person finds that the baby or young child will gradually feel reassured and start to relax, to explore the environment and to play. The children's emotional needs are gradually being met, he or she is beginning to relax and feel more secure in the surroundings. Whilst having used these examples, it must be stressed that, thankfully, such responses are heard far less than prior to 2012. The research and publications of Elfer, Goldschmied, Gerhardt, Goouch and Powell, to name but a few, have explored the Key Person Approach and its effects on children and parents. The effects on Key Persons are covered in more detail in Chapter 3.

Throughout the book you are encouraged to deepen your knowledge and under-standing of children's emotional needs through reflections related to your own settings and practice, through provocations and case studies that are presented in each chapter. You are also given situations like that in the example above to reflect on and relate to similar practical situations you may have encountered in your setting or in how you speak to the children. Is it the way you were spoken to as a child or has it been learned since, when you are with groups of friends? You are encouraged to extend your own learning to include information about theorists and create stronger links to your observations of your Key Children, to your practi-cal experiences and the experiences of the children and parents you are involved with in your workplace. You are also encouraged to consider the impact of your own cultures, values and childhood experiences when working in your settings. This is closely linked to recent and past research into the development of the brain, from the moment of conception, and the influences of not only the Mother's health and wellbeing but also the physical environment. Consideration is given to the effects of exposure to our modern lifestyle, including the revolutionary effects of technology.

The following paragraphs outlining the five chapters in this book provide a brief introduction to and revision of subjects and theories linked to emotional needs of very young children that are discussed in more detail in each of the relevant chapters. Given that children's development is holistic all chapters are strongly linked. Your prior knowledge of attachment theory, neuroscience, the role of all adults and multidisciplinary teams and your professionalism are acknowledged. Ensuring the child is kept at the centre of our focus is reinforced whilst introducing broader aspects of the emotional needs of each child. The book includes references to the history of childcare and education, particularly linked to attachment theory and the role of the Key Person. It includes the changing attitudes of theorists, Early Years Practitioners, Early Years Experts and Government towards children during their Early Years, including some international perspectives. This ultimately sup-ports the focus on the emotional needs of children and their mental and physical wellbeing. It encourages practitioners and students to think about times when they have felt insecure, to reflect on their feelings and relate these feelings to the emo-tional needs of the children in their settings. Consideration is given to the reasons for prolonged emotional insecurity. There is a very strong emphasis on meeting the needs of each child, the importance of the Key Person and of working closely with parents to ensure that children and parents feel valued.

Although the focus is on the emotional needs of babies and young children rather than emotional development, the overarching principles and the section on personal social and emotional development in the Early Years Foundation Stage Framework are included here by way of revision.

Overarching principles

Four guiding principles should shape practice in early years settings. These are:

- every child is a **unique** child, who is constantly learning and can be resilient, capable, confident and self-assured

- children learn to be strong and independent through **positive relationships**

- children learn and develop well in **enabling environments,** in which their experiences respond to their individual needs and there is a strong partnership between practitioners and parents and/or carers

- **children develop and learn in different ways** (see "the characteristics of effective teaching and learning" at paragraph 1.9) and at **different rates.** The framework covers the education and care of all children in early years provision, including children with special educational needs and disabilities.

(EYFS 2017 p. 4)

Personal, social and emotional development

Self-confidence and self-awareness: children are confident to try new activities, and say why they like some activities more than others. They are confident to speak in a familiar group, will talk about their ideas, and will choose the resources they need for their chosen activities. They say when they do or don't need help.

Managing feelings and behaviour: children talk about how they and others show feelings, talk about their own and others' behaviour, and its consequences, and know that some behaviour is unacceptable. They work as part of a group or class, and understand and follow the rules. They adjust their behaviour to different situations, and take changes of routine in their stride.

Making relationships: children play co-operatively, taking turns with others. They take account of one another's ideas about how to organise their activity. They show sensitivity to others' needs and feelings, and form positive relationships with adults and other children.

(EYFS 2017 p. 11)

Keep these sections from the EYFS (2017) in mind as you read through the introduction to each chapter. Can you see any mention of the emotional needs of children? They certainly say that children should develop their personal, social and emotional skills, but how are these skills going to develop if the children's emotional needs are not being met by their significant carers?

Chapter 1: Development of the brain in relation to the emotional needs of very young children

Neuroscience is a very important area of research that over the last three decades has provided all professionals working with very young children with strong evidence of the development of the brain in the first two years of life. This chapter commences by presenting information about the development of the brain from conception, including reference to the changes that occur during puberty. The anatomy of the brain and the principal brain cells, neurons, is included and also the functions of the different areas of the brain are identified. The development of ways in which neural pathways are formed very rapidly in the first two years of life and also the changes that occur when children experience life changing events or do not experience a loving, nurturing environment are discussed. The importance of Mother/Child interactions, eye-contact and proto-conversations (Trevarthen 2002, 2004) are described, discussed and explored. The effects of child abuse and the health of the Mother prior to pregnancy and during the ante and post-natal periods are included. Issues that may arise from post-natal depression are discussed as Early Years Practitioners may well be the first persons to, perhaps, identify the fact that the Mother is unwell. Postnatal depression that affects the ability of the baby and Mother to form a secure attachment because the Mother does not respond to the baby's cues, does not always present immediately after the birth of a baby. The effects of secure and insecure attachment, on the development of the brain, are included as well as being referred to in Chapter 2.

Chapter 2: Attachment theory

This chapter commences with references to the work and research into attachment by Bowlby and Ainsworth and then explores subsequent research that has opposed or questioned some of these earlier theories and findings. Attachment theory researched by Bowlby has been revisited by other researchers and acknowledged as being important, but he has been criticised, by some, because at first, he focused on the Mother as the prime carer and did not acknowledge that children could attach to other significant first carers. Later in his research, Bowlby did acknowledge that babies could form attachments to a person other than the Mother and to more than one person. Neuroscientific research in the 1980s and 1990s provided substantive evidence that Bowlby's theory of attachment was correct. Insecure attachments, identified by Ainsworth, were found to have a profound effect on the development of the brain.

Students are encouraged to critique and analyse the different viewpoints, especially in relation to the development of the brain. Short definitions of attachment, the strange situation, a secure base, different styles of attachment and some of the causes of the differing styles are included. The inability to form a strong attachment when a Mother has ill health or has not experienced attachment with her own Mother is discussed. The importance of sensitively managed transitions is included through discussions about and analysis of different situations or anecdotes, reflections and case studies. Students are encouraged to reflect on the styles of attachment thought to have been identified in children attending their settings and how these issues were addressed. Following their reflections, they are asked if they would manage the issues differently in future. International perspectives on attachment are suggested for further study for the students.

Chapter 3: Key Persons: adults' responses to children

Given this very important aspect of your role one chapter is devoted to exploring the different aspects of the Role of the Key Person. Within this chapter there are discussions about the importance of employing well qualified, experienced, caring staff in all Early Years' settings.

> The importance for young children of their emotional experience at nursery as a central part of the goals of emotional well-being, confident playful exploration, effective thinking and learning, making friends and participating in groups is now widely accepted in early years care and education policy in England and Wales (DfES 2007; DoE 2011)
>
> (Elfer 2012 p. 129)

The role of the Early Years' Practitioner as a Key Person is presented very much from the practical point of view but creates strong links to theory, planning and provision within the settings and the EYFS Framework. Students are encouraged to reflect upon the children in their settings, consider peer observations that have been completed and analyse the responses of adults when working with children. The use and importance of in-depth child observations used when planning the environment and planning for each individual child to ensure that individual developmental needs are met, are strongly reinforced. The chapter includes an exploration of ways to create a calm, welcoming, secure environment where individual emotional needs, play and individual learning needs are valued and responded to. There are strong links to Chapter 2, Attachment theory and Chapter 4 on Working with Parents where the management of transitions is discussed.

Key Workers were gradually introduced in many professions such as Social Work and Nursing during the 1970s and, as discussed in Chapter 3, this role was seen, at first, as more of a managerial and procedural role than as providing for the emotional needs of children. The development of the role of the Key Person followed on from the development and implementation of the Birth to Three Framework (2003) and subsequently the introduction of the Early Years Foundation Stage (EYFS) Framework (2008). In both documents the importance of responding to the emotional needs of each baby and very young child was addressed. Each child, it was suggested, should have a Key Person who would be responsible for their care and education when in a childcare setting. Allocating a Key Person to each baby or young child became mandatory in 2012 when the EYFS was revised. This is discussed in detail in Chapter 3.

Key Person EYFS 3.27.

Each child must be assigned a key person. Their role is to help ensure that every child's care is tailored to meet their individual needs (in accordance with paragraph 1.10), to help the child become familiar with the setting, offer a settled relationship for the child and build a relationship with their parents.

(EYFS 2017 3.27 pp. 22–23)

However, through experience over many years, it is still evident that although Key Persons have been allocated, there are some difficulties with this system for the Key Person. This situation was identified through research by Elfer et al. (2003) but continues to be an issue in many settings, Elfer (2008 – TACTYC Conference and 2012) is discussed in detail in Chapter 3, which also looks at the effects of children experiencing care in multiple settings and the impact of poverty.

Chapter 4: Working with parents

Forming collaborative partnerships and easily accessible, strong lines of communication with parents is one of the most important roles of the Key Person. Listening to and actually hearing parents' requests and concerns and ensuring that routines are followed are priorities. Ensuring that parents and their children are valued, especially acknowledging the knowledge that each parent or carer has about their child, is imperative. The opportunity for reflection and discussion about the different experiences Early Years' Practitioners may have when working with parents and their children is included to ensure that students are able to critique and analyse their relationships with the baby or young child and their parent or carer in order to improve Parental Partnerships in their settings.

Chapter 5: The effects of different cultures experienced by very young children

This chapter commences with definitions of culture, of which there are many because the concept is very confusing, as is mentioned in Chapter 5. It considers the many different cultures that all children encounter during their early childhood. These cultures include the culture of the home, their extended families, the culture within the setting or settings they may attend and the impact of different cultural experiences that the Early Years Practitioners may bring to the setting. The concept of mindfulness is introduced in relation to 'paying more attention the present moment – to your own thoughts and feelings, and the world around you' (NHS 2016). Therefore, not only the effects of cultures but moods, health, expectations, government initiatives etc. are considered. International perspectives are considered in relation to the curriculum and the attitudes to learning within different cultures and the different types of childcare provision. Consideration is given to the effects of the different styles of parenting, parents' differing attitudes and the impact of modern technology that has contributed hugely to change in our culture and to the increase in the number of adolescents experiencing Mental Health problems, for example, self-harming.

Chapter 5 should be read in conjunction with the preceding Chapters 1–4 because culture impacts on all aspects of life, of the home and of the Early Years setting or settings that a baby or child attends. One of the main concerns covered is the experience of an immigrant child who has English as a second language or who has never been exposed to the English Language. The fact that this is not only an issue of the spoken language but also of the difference in cultures between the home and the setting is addressed. The development of language and literacy skills through the use of songs and rhymes that include numeracy and physical development through movement of the body is explored at some length.

Play is also considered in relation to the debate about indoor and outdoor play and the benefits of outdoor play in opposition to staying indoors all day, especially when computers, mobile phones or tablets are being used.

The impact that technology has had on global culture and on the mental health of children and adolescents is discussed.

This introduction provides an overview of the subjects covered in relation to the emotional needs of babies and young children. The words 'emotional needs' have been used frequently in the introduction and are used very frequently in the first five chapters. Before you begin to read the chapters, it would be helpful for you all to consider the definitions of emotions and emotional need. You are all able to provide a long list of feelings or emotions. They are usually divided into positive and negative emotions. Given that it is the negative emotions that give cause for concern because they affect the development of the brain, can you imagine the negative effects those ill babies that I wasn't allowed to pick up were exposed to? Bring the discussion into Early Years Settings, consider how new children are feeling when they have their first session in your setting. Consider how children who have English as their second language feel?

The Oxford Dictionary defines emotion as a *strong feeling or intuition such as love or fear.*

Emotions related to new situations and abuse include:

Anxiety, fear, stress, insecurity, grumpiness, worry, sadness, tearfulness, loneliness, abandonment, anger, distress, misery and bewilderment.

Provided with the right conditions of a warm, welcoming environment, a Key Person who already knows about the baby or young child and their family, one who is able to respond by smiling, listening, hearing and providing for their individual needs and one who gives the baby or child and their parents time to settle, these negative emotions will gradually disappear and be replaced with positive emotions and the innate desire to communicate, play and learn. The fact that the negative emotions are not present for extended periods of time means that the effects of these emotions are negligible, in fact they are emotions that can help with our innate desire for survival.

Should a baby or young child have been abused or exposed to long term conditions where they feel unloved and unsettled, emotions will be stronger and more deep seated. They could include:

depression, worthlessness, jealousy, frustration, rejection, envy, emptiness, fear, feeling used, abused, cheated or unwanted, shame, embarrassment, guilt, confusion, regret, betrayal, anguish, feeling distraught or threatened, isolation and nervousness.

The effects of these negative emotions need not be everlasting even when a baby or young child has experienced long term separation or abuse. However, it will depend on the severity of the abuse and the future care and understanding that they receive. Be prepared to observe the babies and young children carefully, check for changes in behaviour, signs of regression and becoming withdrawn. Remember that although safeguarding has not been detailed in the book, all Early Years Practitioners have a duty to safeguard the children with whom they are working. Focusing on emotional need before being concerned about social and emotional development will enable social and emotional development to gradually take place.

Your role in Early Years is so important!

Further reading

Taggart, G (2011) Don't we care? The ethics and emotional labour of early years profession-alism in *Early Years, An International Journal of Research and Development*, Ed. TACTYC Oxon: Taylor Francis Group, Routledge. This paper provides food for thought about the fact that 'Care' in the Early Years Profession is not viewed as professional when it is in profes-sions such as Nursing.

References

Bowlby, J (1965) 2nd Ed *Child Care and the Growth of Love*, London: Penguin

Bowlby, J (1988/2005) *A Secure Base*, London: Routledge Classic

Comenius, J A (1628–1632) The Whole Art of Teaching, (http://www.froebelweb.org/web7005.html accessed 13 December 2017

DfE (2017) *The Statutory Framework for the Early Years Foundation Stage*, Runcorn: DfE, accessed on line March 2017

DfES (2002) *Birth to Three Matters*, London: DfES Publications

DfES (2007) *The Early Years Foundation Stage*, London: DfES Publications

DoE (2011) Response to the Tickell Review of the Early Years Foundation Stage London: DoE

Elfer, P (2008) *Facilitating intimacy in the care of children under three attending full time nursery*: unpublished doctoral dissertation. UK: University of East London. Findings were shared with delegates at the TACTYC Conference 2008

Elfer, P (2012) Emotion in nursery work: Work Discussion as a model of professional reflec-tion in *Early Years an International Journal of Research and Development*, Volume 32, No 2, July 2012 Ed. TACTYC Oxon: Routledge, Taylor and Francis Group

Elfer, P, Goldschmied, E and Selleck, D (2003) *Key Persons in the Nursery*, London: David Fulton

Garhart Mooney, C (2000) *Theories of Childhood* St Paul, MN: Redleaf Press

Gerhardt, S (2004) *Why Love Matters*, East Sussex: Brunner-Routledge

Holmes, J (2001) *The Search for the Secure Base*, East Sussex: Brunner-Routledge

Ofsted Report (2017) Bold beginnings: The Reception curriculum in a sample of good and outstanding primary schools: London: Ofsted Gov.uk accessed on-line 13 December 2017

Quan-McGimpsey, S, Kuczynski, L, Brophy, K (2011) Early education teachers' conceptualizations and strategies for managing closeness in child care: The personal domain in *Journal of Early Childhood Research* 9: 232 originally published online 21 April 2011 ECR: Sage, accessed on line 13 December 2017

Scott, K (2017) Response to the Ofsted report on Bold Beginnings, *in Nursery World* (8 December 2017), accessed on-line 13 December 2017

TACTYC (2017) A Response to Ofsted's (2017) report, Bold beginnings: The Reception curriculum in a sample of good and outstanding primary schools by TACTYC (Association for Professional Development in Early Years). December 2017 accessed on-line 13 December 2017

Taggart, G (2011) Don't we care? The ethics and emotional labour of early years professionalism in *Early Years, An International Journal of Research and Development*, Ed. TACTYC Oxon: Taylor Francis Group, Routledge

Trevarthen, C (2002) Learning in Companionship in *Education in the North: The Journal of Scottish Education New Series*, No. 10, 2002 pp. 16–25

Trevarthen, C (2004, July) *Making Friends with Infants* Paper presented at Pen Green Conference: Northampton

Websites

http://www.froebelweb.org/web7005.html accessed 13 December 2017

www.nhs.uk/Conditions/stress-anxiety-depression/Pages/mindfulness.aspx accessed Dec 2017

Development of the brain in relation to the emotional needs of very young children

> **Key themes in this chapter**
>
> After reading this chapter you should be able to:
>
> ■ Understand the development of the brain from conception through to five years of age
>
> ■ Discuss the importance of the health and wellbeing of the Mother during antenatal and postnatal periods
>
> ■ Consider the impact on the brain of infections and trauma (accidents)
>
> ■ Discuss the effects of child abuse on brain development
>
> ■ Begin to relate and discuss behaviours exhibited by young children that may have been caused by interruptions in brain development
>
> ■ Reflect on and articulate the importance of in-depth observations in relation to children's emotional development, emotional needs and their all-round development, including providing for their individual needs within your different settings
>
> ■ Analyse and critique the importance of understanding the development of the brain.

Introduction

Neuroscience is a very important area of research which, over the last three decades, has provided all professionals working with very young children with strong evidence of rapid brain development in the first years of life. This chapter provides an overview of the development of the brain from conception through to five years of age and beyond and discusses the ways in which the neural pathways are formed. Reference is made to the changes that occur during puberty and adulthood and to the changes that have been found to occur when children experience life changing events and, or, do not experience a loving, nurturing environment. The effects of child abuse, the health of the Mother prior to pregnancy, during the ante, peri- and post-natal periods are introduced. Issues that may arise from post-natal depression are discussed because Early Years Practitioners may well be the first persons to, perhaps, identify the fact that a Mother is unwell. The importance of Mother to Child and Child to Mother interactions, eye-contact and proto-conversations, linked to the work of Trevarthen (2002, 2004) is presented. Some aspects of attachment are referred to and lead into the chapter on Attachment theories, both past and present. One essential point to make here is, that whilst research by neuroscientists is increasing our knowledge of brain development and the effects of our lives and experiences on this development, a holistic approach to childcare and education must still be maintained. It must also be remembered that brain development continues well after a child's third birthday. Moss (2014) provides food for thought here.

> Let's bring neuroscience into the story. But let's not go overboard
>
> (Moss 2014 p. 22)

In some respects, this quote may sound contradictory to the points being made in this introduction and within the content of the chapter. However, it is so important that Early Years Practitioners retain a balanced view and reflect on their practice and incidents that may arise during their working days. It is essential to use your powers of observation, recording and reflection to ensure that you maintain an objective approach to all aspects of your care and education during your time with the children, parents and other professionals. Yes, the development of the brain and the formation of neural pathways is vitally important, but we must remember not to focus entirely on the brain. Meade (2000) wrote about the importance of the earliest years in relation to brain development.

> There is a convergence of findings from neuroscience, cognitive science, development psychology and early childhood education research. Generally, there is agreement that enriched environments such as are found in high quality early childhood settings facilitate the adaptive changes to children's brains. The enrichment of social relationships – of adult – child interactions – is especially important, remembering of course that the brain is malleable and the changes in response to relationship experience can be both positive and negative for the child.
>
> (Meade (2000) cited in Roberts 2010 p. 5)

Every interaction you as practitioners have with the children in your settings will be helping this process. The following section on the development of the brain and situations that may affect this development will help to assist your observational and reflective skills. It will provide you with information to consider should you have concerns about the development and progress of a child.

The development of the brain

You will already know that from the point of conception when the sperm enters the ovum very rapid cell division commences, with differentiation into the different cell types. The initial development of the cardiac system, including cardiac muscle, the beginnings of the skeletal system, which includes cartilage, and the nervous system, including the creation of neurons, all occurs during the first three months of pregnancy, known as the first trimester.

Figure 1.1 shows the development of the brain and spinal cord from the neural tube at 3 weeks through to birth. It is possible to see, in Figure 1.1, the

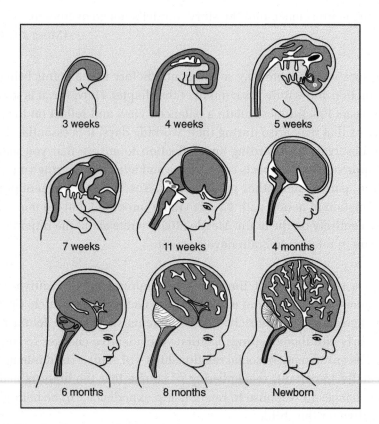

Figure 1.1 The development of the brain during pregnancy.

way that the brain develops in complexity very quickly and that as early as eleven weeks' gestation the spinal cord, the brain stem and the cerebral cortex/ neocortex are already forming and relatively well defined. The brain can be seen developing in what Carter describes as a bulb like way, at the top of the neural tube. It is evident that by the time the baby is born the brain has increased in density and developed complex bulges (gyri) and valleys (sulci) (Carter,1998 and 2010).

Compare the image of the newborn brain in Figure 1.1 with the image of the Evolution-Designed Brain in Figure 1.2. Take into account the fact that in Figure 1.2 the internal view of one hemisphere is shown, not an external view as in Figure 1.1.

Figure 1.2 has the title 'the Evolution-Designed Brain.' This is because it is thought that the human brain has gradually evolved from the basic neural tube still present in fish, through the simple spinal cord and brain required by reptiles. From this stage it developed into the limbic system of early mammals and finally the complex human brain with the ever-changing cerebral cortex that humans have today. (Carter 2010). All of the different areas are still present in the human brain and can be clearly seen in Figure 1.1, as the brain develops.

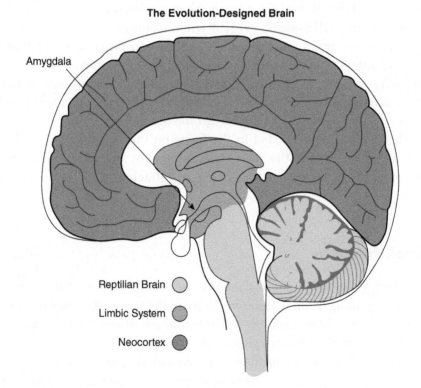

The Evolution-Designed Brain

Amygdala

Reptilian Brain

Limbic System

Neocortex

Figure 1.2 The evolution-designed brain showing the reptilian brain, the limbic brain and the neocortex.

The evolutionary development of the different areas of the brain is clearly defined here using colour-coding. It can be seen that the shape closely resembles the image of the brain of a newborn:

- The Reptilian Brain controls reflex actions, breathing, sleeping, waking and the heartbeat, all of which are required for survival (Pally 2000). It also includes the cerebellum which controls movement, and which, was the 'main brain' (Carter 2010) of mammals prior to mammalian evolution and the development of the neocortex.

- The Limbic System, which includes the amygdala, controls emotions, memory, nursing, care and play, sometimes referred to as 'our emotional brain'. (OECD 2007).

- The Neocortex gradually increased in size as humans evolved. This area controls intelligence, language, movement, vision and reasoning, described by Pally as the 'executive centre of the brain' (Pally 2000 p. 4). The neocortex, also known as the cerebral cortex, is the main part of the brain that receives messages via the neural pathways (see Figures 1.2 and 1.3) and responds to the demands from within the body and the different environmental experiences of each baby throughout life. It, with the cerebellum and amygdala, controls who we are, as will become evident when examining Figure 1.4 where the functions of the brain are illustrated, and, as you progress through this and related chapters. The neocortex is the part of the brain that has evolved. It has a property, often described as 'plasticity', maintained throughout life, that enables changes to occur. However, plasticity within the brain is at its highest level in the early years, from birth until the age of three years. It is these findings that have, obviously, led to the focus on the development of the brain and experiences within the early years, especially the early interactions and development of a secure attachment. Secure attachment is discussed in depth in Chapter 2.

Areas of the brain

The diagram below, Figure 1.3 gives a more detailed view of the structure of brain, it is beginning to show the complexity of the brain. The cerebral cortex has been subdivided and two endocrine glands that are situated within the brain are included; these are the pituitary gland and the pineal gland.

Whilst the brain is being considered in some detail, how are the messages transferred from different parts of the body to the brain? The nervous system is divided in two parts, the central nervous system (CNS) which consists of the brain and

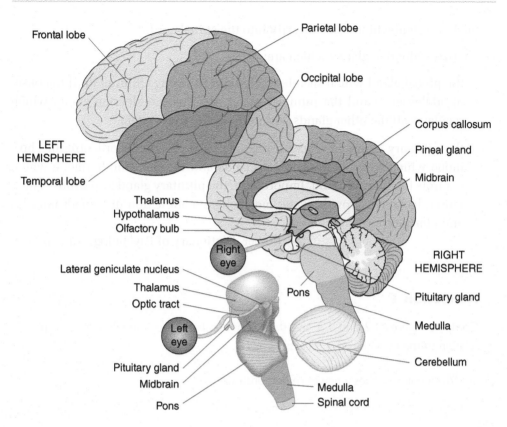

Figure 1.3 The areas of the brain.

the spinal cord and the peripheral nervous system (PNS) which is formed of the nerves that branch out from the brain and spinal cord to supply and connect to all parts of the body. This allows for the transmission of electrical impulses from our finger tips, skin, limbs, muscles and organs to the appropriate area of the brain where the electrical impulses are received and interpreted. However, the anatomy and functions of the brain are the main concentration in this chapter because the development of the brain is very closely related to the emotional needs of very young children, as stated above and in Chapter 2.

Figure 1.3 above shows:

■ the right and left hemispheres which are, when not illustrated as two separate hemispheres, joined together by the corpus callosum which allows stimuli to be transmitted across from one hemisphere of the brain to the other;

■ the four lobes, the frontal, the parietal, the occipital and the temporal, which form the cerebral cortex;

■ the cerebellum;

- the brain stem which leads directly into the spinal cord;

- the two endocrine glands which are:

  - the pineal gland which secretes melatonin in young children until the onset of adolescence and the pituitary gland, the major endocrine gland, which regulates all the other glands within the endocrine system.

  - the pituitary gland produces hormones such as adrenocorticotrophic hormone which controls the adrenal glands and thyrotrophic hormone which controls the thyroid gland. Importantly, the pituitary gland also controls ovulation, lactation, growth, water metabolism, contraction of smooth muscles and uterine contractions.

(Reber, Dictionary of Psychology 1995 p. 573)

Reflection 1

Compare Figures 1.2 and 1.3 and then consider the development of the brain in relation to the evolutionary process.

- Which reflexes does a newborn demonstrate?

- Do we retain all the reflexes we are born with?

- Do some of our repeated daily actions become reflex actions?

- How has the human brain evolved?

- Observe babies in your settings and identify the reflexes that babies use.

Further information can be found in 'Mapping the Mind', Carter (2010). There is also interesting information about 'mapping the brain', using your hand and forearm (see Rose, Gilbert, and Richards, 2016, who relate the mapping to the work of Siegal 2012).

The reflexes that are present at birth include the rooting reflex, the sucking reflex, the startle reflex and the walking reflex. Babies also have the ability to swim under water as can be easily observed and experienced during a water-birth. You will remember that some of these reflexes disappear during the first few weeks of a baby's life such as the walking reflex, the startle reflex and the ability to swim underwater. This is because these particular functions are not used until later in the baby's development, when they may be re-learnt. You may be saying or thinking that we all react if we are startled. We do, but we do not fling our arms out, we tend to jump. The functions of the different areas of the brain will now be discussed.

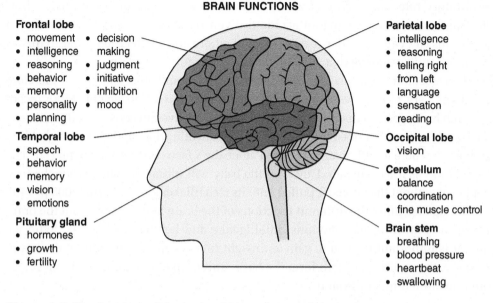

Figure 1.4 The functions of the brain within each area of the brain.

Functions of the brain

Whilst there are areas of the brain that control specific actions and knowledge, it must be remembered and appreciated that the brain and spine, the Central Nervous System, and the Peripheral Nervous System do not function independently; they work as a 'whole'. The four lobes in the cerebral cortex, the frontal, the parietal, the temporal and the occipital lobes, as you can see in Figure 1.4, have joint responsibilities in that more than one area has responsibility for similar functions, for example:

▨ memory is controlled in both the frontal and temporal lobes

▨ intelligence is controlled in the frontal and parietal lobes

▨ vision is controlled in the occipital and temporal lobes.

In Figure 1.4 the temporal lobe is labelled as controlling emotions. However, the amygdala in Figure 1.2, in close proximity to the limbic brain, is also involved in the control of emotions. The frontal lobe helps to regulate emotions by controlling the functions of intelligence, behaviour, decision making, inhibition, empathy and mood, this is termed 'executive functioning'.

The brain stem controls breathing, blood pressure, heartbeat and swallowing – actions that are automatic. You do not normally think about these functions unless you are experiencing discomfort, or, for example, you have been exercising when you will notice a rise in your heart and respiration rates. The heart rate and respiratory rate can often rise when experiencing unpleasant situations such as hearing bad news or seeing an accident. Even imagining or reading about such situations can cause similar responses. Blakemore and Frith (2005) refer to this as an *autonomic response* that is processed in the emotional brain.

The cerebellum controls balance, fine motor skills and co-ordination. It therefore functions very closely with the frontal lobe that controls movement. More recent research has suggested that the cerebellum may be involved in conditioned responses, such as those first described by Pavlov with the salivating dogs and now the 'eye-blink response', where a puff of air is directed at a baby's face whilst a tone is played. The baby blinks as it feels the air. However, the baby will ultimately blink when the tone is played without the air being puffed onto its face (Blakemore and Frith 2005 p. 140).

Having identified the different functions of the brain and spoken about the brain being in control of our emotions, intelligence and behaviours, that is, 'who we are', it is important for you to gain an insight into the microstructure of the brain. Namely, the 'neurons' which form the basic unit of the brain and ensure messages are transmitted to and from it.

Structure and functions of neurons

Neurons are cells formed of an axon with axon tips, a cell body which includes the nucleus and dendrites extending from the cell body. These structures can be seen below in Figure 1.5.

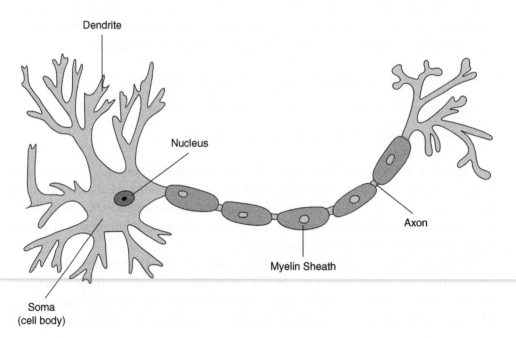

Figure 1.5 Diagram of a neuron: brain cell.

An axon and its axon tips belonging to one neuron form structures known as synapses with the dendrites belonging to adjacent neurons. Impulses pass from the axon tips to the dendrites, creating the connections required to ensure that signals are passed from the area of stimulation through to the brain. Each neuron is thought to connect with up to 10,000 of its neighbours (Carter 1998), whilst Gopnick, Meltzoff and Kuhl (2001) and Shore (1997) each speak of a single neuron having approximately 2,500 synapses at birth and 15,000 by the age of three.

Illustration of axons connecting to the next set of dendrites via synapses

The connection of one neuron to the next is enabled by the release of chemicals called neurotransmitters, secreted at each synapse (see Figure 1.6) and is known as neurotransmission, also referred to as synaptogenesis by Blakemore and Frith (2005). They, Blakemore and Frith, highlight the fact that within the visual cortex synaptogenesis is very rapid in babies at around two to three months and peaks between eight and ten months, after which time the activity decreases. This results in the number of synaptic connections within the visual cortex gradually declining until the age of ten years. The number of synaptic connections then remains relatively stable throughout adulthood. Blakemore and Frith also discuss the different

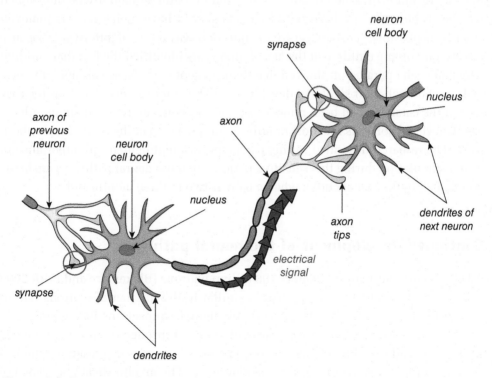

Figure 1.6 Diagram of two neurons showing a connection between an axon and a dendrite.

rates of synaptogenesis within the frontal lobe, stating that 'this occurs later in the development of the brain and continues throughout adolescence'. The synaptic connections are protected by the formation of the myelin sheath which surrounds the neurons. This process is known as myelination.

Reflection 2

Consider the information above regarding the rapid increase in the number of synapses being formed in the visual cortex and relate it to the development of babies' visual skills that you observe:

■ What is the focal length for a newborn?

■ What are they able to do at the age of two to three months?

■ Observe two babies, one of this age and one aged ten months, record their actions and then relate your findings to their visual development.

■ Which theorists you have studied previously may agree or disagree with your findings?

Blakemore and Frith (2005 p. 29) cite research by Daphne Maurer who questioned whether babies who are born with cataracts should have their cataracts removed as early as possible? The answer to this question was not straightforward, because research involving children at the age of nine years identified the fact that children who had been operated on showed that their perception of faces was not quite normal, even though their sight had developed quickly after surgery. This was the case even if the cataracts had been removed as early as between two and six months of age. The visual cortex is the most rapidly developing area of the brain in a newborn baby. The research described in this paragraph has highlighted the importance of visual stimulation during this sensitive period when the neural pathways are being established in the visual cortex when a baby is two to three months old.

Continued development of the neural pathways

A baby is born with approximately 100 billion neurons (Blakemore and Frith 2005 and Carter 1998, 2010). This number is similar to the number of neurons within an adult brain; however, there are very few neural connections in the brain of a newborn baby. Neural connections are only created through continued, repeated stimulation and use of pathways causing a process known as myelination which is the formation of the myelin sheath, see Figure 1.6. The myelin sheath is formed of a fatty white substance that surrounds the axon of nerve cells, forming an electrically insulating layer. These connections, forming a network of neural pathways, become most dense by the age of six years (Carter 1998, 2010), however, if the connections are not used, they gradually die. This does not mean that new neural pathways are not created after the age of six years. New neural pathways continue to be created throughout our lives but do not increase or decrease significantly in number. The changes in the neural pathways occur in response to changes in environment and life events, particularly those affecting emotional and cognitive experiences. This ability of the brain to change the neural pathways as they are used or not used is described as 'plasticity', as has already been mentioned earlier in the chapter. These changes and the causes of the changes are discussed further within this chapter and in Chapters 2, 3 and 5.

As you have been reading about and studying the development and structure of the brain you will have recognized the importance and complexity of the brain's structure and functions. Until recently, because of its important function and complexity, research on the brain has been carried out using animals, not humans, unless information was discovered during post mortem examinations, as discussed by Blakemore and Frith (2005), Carter (1998) and Shore (1997). This situation has changed with the advent of advanced technology including Magnetic Resonance Imaging (MRI) and Positron Emission Topography (PET) scans that enable neuroscientists to observe the normal functioning brain and to identify and diagnose malfunctions and structural abnormalities within the brain, and conditions such as haemorrhages or tumours as well as gauging the size of the brain and the density of the neural connections. These scans can be supported by Electroencephalography (EEG), where the brainwaves are measured, and more recently by Magnetoencephalography (MEG) which uses the magnetic pulses caused by neuronal oscillation (Carter 1998, 2010), providing neuroscientists and physicians with information about activity within the brain.

The illustration in Figure 1.7 shows the results of MRI scans across the ages from birth to adulthood which support information relating to synapse density.

Synapse density over time

When comparing the density of the synapses as seen in Figure 1.7 below, in the scan of the newborn it is evident that very few neural pathways are present, but by the age of one month there is an obvious increase in the number of neural pathways. It is then apparent that the formation of neural pathways has accelerated between the age of nine months and two years, whilst it appears that the density of synapses in the adult scan has reduced. This is due to the process of natural *pruning* (Carter 2010, Gerhardt 2004, Gopnick, Meltzoff and Kuhl 2001) – those

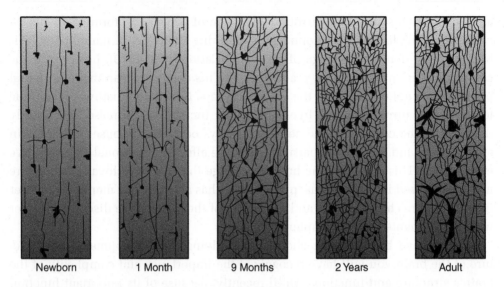

Newborn   1 Month   9 Months   2 Years   Adult

Figure 1.7 The increase in synapse density from newborn through to adulthood.

Source: Adapted from Corel, J L. The postnatal development of the human cerebral cortex. Cambridge, MA: Harvard University Press; 1975. http://www.urbanchildinstitute.org/why-0-3/baby-and-brain accessed 31 December 2016.

synapses that are no longer used 'dying off'. However, the remaining synapses will gradually be strengthened, as can be seen in the brain scan of the adult and has already been referred to earlier in the chapter. This process can be compared to other areas of nature such as trees and bushes that also need to be pruned regularly (Gopnick, Meltzoff and Kuhl 2001). By pruning excess growth, the remaining stems and branches strengthen, which results in the production of substantial, healthy crops. This is the very positive outcome of 'pruning' for plants, as it is for 'pruning' the human brain. The effects of insufficient stimulation, lack of exercise, poor environment, genetics and lack of responses or inappropriate responses by adults on the emotional needs of very young children and the possible effects on the development of the brain will be explored in more detail in Chapters 2, 3, 5 and 6.

In Figure 1.7 there is no scan of an adolescent's brain. However, it is now well known that the adolescent brain, especially the frontal cortex, is very different before and after puberty. There is no increase in the size of the cerebral cortex but there is an increase in the myelination of axons, which may increase the speed of transmission along these neurons following puberty (Blakemore and Frith (2005). Research in 2003, cited by Blakemore and Frith, confirmed that there was a decrease in grey matter within the frontal lobes before and during puberty but that myelination, the formation of white matter, continued right up to the age of 60.

This evidence again reinforces the importance of the care and interaction that is needed when working with very young children, the importance for practitioners of responding to each child's learning and emotional needs through accurate observation, appropriate communication, appointing key persons and the provision of appropriate resources.

Continue to study Figure 1.4 to create a chart that shows the lobes where the different functions are controlled. Search the internet and refer to the further reading to find more complex diagrams and more in-depth information about the functions of the brain. You may also refer to the end of this chapter where further reading is suggested. This will enable you to extend your knowledge and understanding of brain development and functions of each area of the brain.

Reflection 3

Consider this statement:
'No part of the human body can function independently'

■ Is this true or false?

■ Are you able to explain the reason for this?

■ How are all parts of the body interrelated?

As Childcare and Early Years' practitioners, along with all other professionals involved in the Health and Wellbeing of very young children;

We need holistic approaches based on the interdependence of body and mind, the emotional and the cognitive

(OECD 2007 p. 8)

This chapter has covered the development and anatomy of the brain, neurons and neural pathways from the time of conception until birth. The rapid development and increasing complexity of the brain and its functions have been considered up to the age of ten years. Reference has also been made to the plasticity of the brain particularly during the Early Years, adolescence and into adulthood. The areas of the brain that are involved with and control emotions have been identified and information is expanded in Chapters 3, 4, 5 and 6 where the focus widens from normal development and natural processes to the impact of life experiences, cultures and the environment. Given that the foetus is in utero for nine months it is essential to consider the health of the Mother before and throughout pregnancy and after the birth of the baby.

The importance of the health and wellbeing of the Mother during the perinatal period

---

Reflection 4

Consider the following statements before reading this section so that the scene is set for considering a Mother's health and wellbeing.

Early brain development establishes a child's social competence, cognitive skills, emotional well-being, language, literacy skills and physical abilities, and is a marker for well-being in school and life resiliency

(Blair, 2002, 'On Track' 21 December 2016)

■ What are your thoughts?

■ How does this make you feel?

■ How important is the health and wellbeing of the Mother?

■ What do we mean by health and wellbeing?

■ What is your role?

As with neuroscience and brain development there has long been a focus on the health and wellbeing, not just of adults but also of children. In the Constitution of the World Health Organisation 1948, complete health and wellbeing is defined as:

Health is a state of complete physical, mental and social well-being and not merely the absence of disease or infirmity.

World Health Organization 1948

United Nations Convention on the Rights of the Child, Article 3 states:

The best interests of the child must be a top priority in all decisions and actions that affect children.

Commencing with our minds focused, initially, on the Mother but also keeping in mind the baby and very young child, it must be the wish of every Mother and person involved in childcare and education, that a healthy baby is born. The ideal is for that baby to develop into a healthy child whose emotions are responded to immediately and appropriately. However, you will be very aware that, sadly, this is not always the situation. Over the past decade, it has become more and more evident that the experiences of the foetus whilst in utero impact on the future.

For many, many years now it has been realized that the newborn baby is not, as John Locke stated, 'an empty slate'. The baby has been exposed to sounds, albeit altered or muffled by being inside the uterus, surrounded by the placenta and amniotic fluid. During scans a baby can be observed with eyes open, sucking fingers and thumbs, kicking and waving arms about; this is technology that was not available when John Locke made the above statement. However, many Mothers will be able to confirm that their babies have reacted to sounds by kicking when startled by a sudden noise such as a bang or loud music being played. Many Mothers will talk to their babies, caress them and sing to them – the beginnings of communication and an introduction to their natural culture.

At the beginning of the chapter the speed of development, cell division and differentiation, was introduced. You read about the development of the brain during the first semester. You revised the fact that nervous system is almost complete by the eleventh week. This is one of the periods of development described by Carter (2010), Gerhardt (2004) and Pally (2000) as critical or sensitive periods. The description 'sensitive' is preferred by many childcare experts and neuroscientists and there is much debate surrounding the focus on these sensitive periods.

Given that the rate of cell division is so fast during the first trimester, it is a time when Health Visitors, Social Workers and many professionals would say a Mother should be taking care of her health and wellbeing either self-initiated or with the help of professionals such as Doctors, Midwives, Health Visitors and Social Workers. Health professionals also include the months leading up to conception as a time when women should consider their health and wellbeing to ensure the health of their baby. Ideally, Mothers-to-be will be healthy and have a strong sense of wellbeing. This, as you are aware, is not always the case. With the increasing knowledge about the importance of a Mother's health and well-being, there is well documented information available in Senior Schools, in Doctors' Surgeries and on-line about educational classes and how to access help and guidance. BUT, although support is available both prenatally and perinatally, is everyone aware of this and does everyone, even if they know about the information, access and take advantage of it? Could this also be a cultural issue? One could argue that there is too much information for prospective parents. There is a long list of dos and don'ts relating to diet, lifestyle, medication, alcohol intake and drugs that is also constantly changing. This, for all parents to be, can be overwhelming. The aim of all professionals working with parents during the perinatal phase of their lives is to ensure that the Mother remains healthy throughout the pregnancy and a healthy baby is born.

There are many reasons why a Mother may feel very anxious/stressed such as:

- Their age, they may feel too young – teenage pregnancy – or may think they are too old.

- They may have financial difficulties when the costs of a new baby would acerbate these issues.

- Their relationship with their partner may not be strong; they may be a single parent. Barlow (2016) identifies the perinatal period and transitions to parenthood as potentially stressful.

- They may worry about the baby, whether it will be healthy, what it will be like in looks and personality, and how, when it arrives, it will affect their life-style.

- Their living conditions may not be suitable for a young baby.

- The Mother or Father may have chronic health problems which may affect the development of the baby.

- The Mother or Father may be taking drugs, alcoholics or smoking heavily.

- There may be a history of genetically transmitted conditions within the extended family which may cause anxieties for both parents.

- Fear of giving birth.

You may now be thinking, 'well that is all very normal to have concerns; most Mothers and Fathers have some of these concerns.' Yes, they do and for most there is a wonderful outcome. However, consideration should now be given to the effects of their anxieties, as listed above, on the newborn child.

Significant sensitive developmental periods have already been identified in the section on the development of the brain as during pregnancy, the first two years of life and again during adolescence. The first two years of life was spoken about by Nolan (2016) during a Sector Endorsed Foundation Degree Early Years Professional Association (SEFDEY) National Meeting as the first 1,000 days of a child's life, i.e. from the point of conception to the second birthday, thus including the first, second and third trimesters. Barlow (2016) speaks about 'certain types of experience' needing to be present. From birth the experiences which should occur are, sight and language-based, as introduced earlier, and those relating to basic sensory and motor functions. If these experiences, referred to by Barlow as 'the biological embedding of social adversity' do not happen during this sensitive developmental period, perhaps because of poor relationships, poor nutrition or unsafe physical or chemical and built environments, that may result in an interaction with the child's genetics, with the result that the brain and other organs do not develop normally. Although, as Barlow (2016) recognises, this processing is not fully understood. It is, however, well documented that a lack of communication, a lack of appropriate responses by the adult to a baby's cries, a lack of physical contact, especially a loving nurturing environment will all affect the development of the brain and the ability to form attachments. This is due to sustained, excessive release of the hormone cortisol, due to high stress levels, when a baby is not responded to. The neural pathways are not developed in the infant's brain resulting in the inability for the baby and Mother to form strong bonds of attachment (Bowlby 1965; 1988, Rose, Gilbert and Richards 2016).

Nicotine from smoking, and drugs such as heroin, cocaine and alcohol, consumed during pregnancy, have severe adverse effects on the development of the placenta and the brain. If the Mother is a drug addict, the newborn baby is often addicted to the drug that has been taken and will display symptoms of withdrawal. One of the main effects of taking drugs such as heroin and cocaine is that they allow high levels of dopamine to be released into the brain, rather than being contained. Dopamine controls a person's 'feel good factor', happiness and pleasure. However, high levels of dopamine can result in a feeling of anxiety, aggression and depression which is related to a drop in the level of seratonin produced. Seratonin is closely linked to Dopamine in that it too, controls levels of happiness; they are both neurotransmitters. Low levels of serotonin cause depression and also affect learning and memory. In a neonate, the symptoms of drug withdrawal normally manifest at any time after delivery from 12 to 72 hours but may not do so for up to 14 days. The length of time for symptoms to arise varies with the drug that has been taken by the Mother. The symptoms observed are generally poor feeding, irritability, inability to be comforted and a high-pitched cry. A high-pitched cry is also a sign of cerebral irritation and other conditions, not just drug withdrawal. Could cerebral irritation be what is occurring during drug withdrawal?

The development of the placenta is mentioned above and is linked to the adverse effects of smoking; a condition known as placental insufficiency may occur. It is a condition where the placenta does not receive a sufficient blood supply to provide the essential blood flow from the placenta through the umbilical cord to the baby. Thus, the baby receives insufficient oxygen and nutrients, often resulting in a very small baby or possibly the death of the baby. This may be because the placenta has not attached fully to the uterus, or has started to detach itself from the uterus.

Placental insufficiency may also be associated with medical conditions in the Mother such as:

- Anaemia

- Diabetes

- High blood pressure

- Smoking

- Some medicines

These conditions have been included to broaden your concept of the difficulties that may affect the Mother and baby around the perinatal period. The previous paragraphs have provided some insight into the effects of the poor health and wellbeing of the Mother on the development of the baby. The effects on the development of the brain have been mentioned along with some of the symptoms that may be observed in the newborn baby. These symptoms are very closely linked to the emotions of the baby, i.e. stress, depression, irritability, the inability to be comforted and a high-pitched cry. A baby's emotions may also be affected by feeding difficulties which will result in feelings of hunger and discomfort through not having one of their very basic needs met. These topics are returned to in Chapters 2 and 4. The importance of the perinatal period and naturally occurring, *sensitive developmental periods*, have already been identified. However, there are external factors such as infections and trauma that may affect the 'normal' development of the brain or damage the brain and impact on the emotions.

Consider the effects of infections and trauma (accidents) on the functioning of the brain and emotional development.

Serious infections that impact on the functioning of the brain, such as meningitis, meningococcal septicaemia, encephalitis and measles may cause varying degrees of regression or prevent further development. These conditions may also prove to be fatal, as you already know. Hence the immunization programmes that now exist to help prevent babies and young children from succumbing to these bacteria and viruses.

Case study I

An example of regression but subsequent recovery was observed in a three-year-old child who had a viral meningitis. The child was very ill on admission to hospital. She was not responding, had a weak high-pitched cry and a condition known as opisthotonos was present. This is a condition where the back curves backwards into the shape of the letter 'C', a sign of severe inflammation of the meninges. However, once provided with the appropriate medication and care the recovery period became very interesting to observe. Once consciousness had been regained, the child moved through the phases of physical development from sitting to crawling to walking again, all within the space of approximately three to four weeks.

Apparently, a full recovery was ultimately made which demonstrates the ability of the brain to recover. It is also worth noting here that the child in this case study had been taken to her GP on three occasions prior to admission to hospital. This situation supports the advice given to parents now, that they should go to hospital if they are convinced that there is something seriously wrong with their baby or young child.

The condition of the child in the case study above was the result of an acquired infection. However, the first experience for most babies when brain damage may occur, is birth. Birth is a long and tortuous journey for all babies and not without some dangers. Does this experience have an impact on the emotional needs of babies? It possibly does because labour is another possible example of an experience for the Mother which might lead to difficulties in bonding with the new baby. This is especially so if the delivery has been long and exhausting, or there have been concerns about the health of the baby. It may also result in some brain damage for the baby, such as a minor or severe cerebral haemorrhage that can result in the baby developing cerebral palsy.

It will now be assumed that the delivery progressed normally and the baby was handed directly to the Mother or Father. In the majority of cases the baby is immediately cuddled, caressed, spoken to and shown the love that it needs. There are examples of the baby being given naked to the Mother so that there can be skin to skin contact. This is known as Kangaroo Care, which is found to assist the attachment process. There may be moments when the baby opens its eye and stares into the face of the parent, the very beginning of stimulation for the visual cortex. Earlier in the chapter you were asked to consider the focal length of vision for a baby of this age. It is about 200 to 300 millimetres; it allows the baby to focus on the Mother's face and for the Mother to gaze into the eyes of the baby when in arms, the baby's head resting in the crook of the Mother's arm (Johnson 2016). This positive response is the beginning of communication, love and nurturing that should continue throughout the child's life, although the modes of communication, love and nurturing will change and develop with the child as it responds, matures and feels secure. The important beginnings of attachment are developing through this close contact and communication, and neural pathways are being formed.

Reflection 5

Consider what it might be like for the baby who does not have these positive experiences and the impact this may have on their emotional development. The baby may not experience the beginnings of communication, cuddles and love when a Mother has been diagnosed as suffering from post-natal depression. A Mother shares the information with you that she has post-natal depression and is on medication.

- How will you provide support for the Mother?

- How will you ensure the baby receives communication, cuddles and love whilst in your setting without undermining the role of the Mother?

- What advice, if any, might you give to the Mother?

It is well documented that humans have a strong desire to communicate (Trevarthen 2011), however if the Mother is feeling depressed and withdrawn, her ability to communicate with her baby will be affected and impact on the baby's ability to form a secure attachment with her. Instead of the baby looking to the Mother for response and communication the baby too will stop trying to communicate. Further information is available in Chapter 2, where Attachment Theory is considered in detail.

An external trauma such as a fall or a road traffic accident may result in a child sustaining a head injury when brain damage may occur. The brain damage may be slight, perhaps resulting in concussion from which a child usually recovers relatively quickly. A child who has sustained a serious head injury may experience future learning difficulties, emotional problems, physical disability, loss of vision or memory loss, may not recover consciousness and may suffer from fitting, dependent upon the area of the brain that is affected. An injury to the frontal lobe of the brain may affect the emotional needs and social, emotional development of a child. The child may subsequently be unable to show empathy towards others. He or she may not be able to understand other children's feelings.

Two examples of trauma directly related to the brain have been written about here. However, as you know, many events throughout life are traumatic at the time, and are described as psychological trauma. Children can become very emotional and upset when they fall over or someone snatches a toy. At the time of these incidents the child's world seems as if it is 'falling apart'. These examples are usually short lived and do not usually affect the child's long term emotional development or have an impact on the developmental processes in the brain. However, if a child experiences long term trauma in the form of abuse or bullying it does have an impact on the process of synaptogenesis. Any form of severe abuse will, or can result in emotional abuse which will affect the development of the brain. Brain scans of children of three years of age who have been abused, when compared with brain scans of children who have developed strong attachments with their parents or carers, have identified that the brain of the abused child is significantly smaller than that of the securely attached child at the same age.

The effects of abuse on the development of the brain

This evidence sends a very powerful message about the effects of child abuse on the process of synaptogenesis and on the size of the brain and the resultant effects on the child's ability to manage their emotions. As you all know, abuse causes many different changes in a child's behaviours. These changes are often the first signs that a child may be experiencing problems in life. You, as a practitioner may be the first person to identify these changes. Therefore, it is very important to be able to identify these behaviours, keep an open mind, record your observations and report your concerns to your senior or the designated person. You have a huge responsibility to 'safeguard' every child in your care. Consider Provocation 1 in relation to your responsibility to 'safeguard' every child in your care and as a revision exercise.

Provocation 1

A neighbour of a young child, aged two years, who attends your setting, asks to speak to you in confidence. The neighbour tells you about an incident when she has heard the child screaming and the child's Mother shouting and crying out 'Don't you hit him.' The screaming and shouting carried on for about half an hour. I am telling you because I am worried for the safety of the child, and, the safety of the Mother. This is not the first time I have heard this. Please can you help?

Consider the way you would manage this situation and what you would do with the information you have received. It is a very difficult situation, it is essential to remain very professional, the information is 'hearsay'. However, it is your duty and responsibility to safeguard all children in your care, as stated above. How would you respond to the neighbour? Who would you share the information with? What would you do with the information? Would you consider observing the young child more closely for any signs of harm or changes in behaviours? Would you speak to the child's parents?

Obviously, you must maintain confidentiality, maintain your professional position and not enter into any form of discussion about the child or their family, with the neighbour. Record the information and place it in a locked file having informed the designated person. Your response to the neighbour, could be, 'thank you very much for letting me know. You may advise the neighbour to contact the police or social services should they have any concerns in the future.

By way of revision there are four main types of abuse:

Physical

Emotional

Neglect

Sexual

However, the impact of domestic violence is now being discussed regularly and should be included when considering a child's changes in behaviour. Domestic abuse may involve psychological, physical, sexual, financial and emotional abuse, usually directed at a parent, which results in emotional abuse for the child. Research has identified the fact that domestic abuse often commences during a Mother's pregnancy. It also found that the incidence is high:

one in six pregnant women will experience domestic violence and 30% of domestic violence starts or worsens during pregnancy.

(midwifery.org.uk accessed 12 January 2017)

The situation is replicated in different parts of the world not just in the United Kingdom. Domestic abuse towards a pregnant woman, if physical, can result in miscarriage, premature birth, foetal injury or death.

Returning to the effects of abuse on a child, the signs and symptoms you might observe are:

- Withdrawal

- Regression

- Bruising

- Unexplained fractures

- Burns

- Loss of appetite

- Loss of weight

- Change of mood

- Aggression

These changes in behaviour highlight the importance of in-depth or longitudinal observations of the children in your setting, particularly if you have identified specific changes in behaviour. You might identify a pattern to the behaviours which could be related to a trigger within the nursery, changes at home such as one parent being away from home or the birth of a new baby. However, the causes may be more worrying, especially if a combination of the above is identified. You will need to use your observations to create an action plan to support the child's emotional needs and their all-round development, including providing for their individual needs within your different settings and in collaboration with their parent/s. If a parent has not reported an injury on arrival in your setting you should, or the manager should, speak to the parent at the end of the child's session. Most importantly you will report your findings and concerns to the designated person, as mentioned above.

Conclusion

The topics covered in this chapter have identified the importance of the experiences and interactions of children from conception, throughout their early years, during adolescence and throughout life. It has included the anatomy of the central nervous system, the brain which is formed of millions of neurons, and the process of myelination from birth to the age of three and beyond. The plasticity of the brain has been discussed in the light of research that has identified the fact that the structure is continuously changing, as has the process of pruning as the neurons and neural pathways are no longer used and new pathway are created.

The areas of the brain have been identified including the functions of each area. The impact of discoveries in neuroscience since the 1990s, enabled by huge advances in technology and recorded by Carter (2010) and Blakemore and Frith (2005), have been included with thoughts about the implications for Early Years Settings and the responsibility of Key Persons when working with babies and very young children. It has included information about the related technology, the development of the brain and conditions that may affect the development of the brain. When reading information about neuroscience it has become apparent that in the beginning, in the 1990s, the response to this new information by many professionals, particularly educationalists and parents, was to ensure that children were provided with a curriculum related to the rapid development of the brain between birth and two years. Many academics such as Gopnick, Meltzoff and Kuhl (2001); Moss (2014); House (2011) raised concerns about the impact this was having on provision and as House identified, '*expecting too much too soon*', from very young children.

The advances of neuroscience have been acknowledged but with warnings about using 'sensitive developmental periods' to ensure children learn as much as possible during these periods, especially from birth to three years. *Learning opportunities need to be available to all ages.* (Blakemore and Frith 2005 p. 35) All professionals must continue to respond to the individual needs of each child to ensure they receive the care and education that is appropriate at that time. To ensure that a child's brain continues to develop well, that each child has a sense of well-being and their emotional needs are being met it remains imperative that you:

- Continue to ensure that you work in collaboration with parents and other professionals who may be involved with a child.

- Observe and assess where the child is and what the child can do rather than identifying what they cannot do.

- Identify each child's interests and use those to extend their learning.

If a child is overstimulated their inbuilt curiosity, desire to explore and problem solve, may be affected. The child may also become stressed, which will affect their all-round development because their emotional and developmental needs are not being met; the level of cortisol released will be high. These themes are returned to and explored in depth in the ensuing chapters. However, with their parents, you, in your role as a Key Person, are supporting the emotional needs of each of your Key Children and ultimately their all-round-development, including the formation of strong neural pathways through response to their individual needs.

Human development hinges on the interplay between nature and nurture.

It was assumed that the genes we are born with determine how our brains develop. Neuroscientists have found that throughout the entire process of development, beginning even before birth, the brain is affected by environmental conditions, including the kind of nourishment, care, surroundings, and stimulation an individual receives. The impact of the environment is dramatic and specific, not merely influencing the general direction of development, but actually affecting how the intricate circuitry of the brain is wired.

(Shore 1997 p. ix)

Further reading

The four texts below have been chosen to help you extend and deepen your learning about neuroscience, the development of and the causes of interruption to the process of development of the brain. Each text provides a different but linked perspective to the impacts that different life experiences have on brain development from conception through to adolescence.

Barlow, J (2016) Improving Relationships in the Perinatal Period: What Works in *AIMH UK Best Practice Guidance (BPG) No 1;* London: AIMH
This text, as the title signifies, is linked to the relationships of Mothers with babies around the antenatal and postnatal periods. It was written in collaboration with the Association of Infant Mental Health and is, therefore, relevant for all professionals working with parents and children around the perinatal period. It has been included to provide you with information that might help you to support Mothers and their children when attending your setting.

Carter, R, (2010), *Mapping the Mind.* London: Weidenfeld & Nicholson (Orion Books Ltd)
Mapping the Mind provides excellent detailed information about the development of the brain from conception through the Early Years and on to adulthood. There are many diagrams showing the structure of the brain and images of scans showing the areas of the brain controlling vision, hearing, emotions, speech etc. It addresses issues related to failure of the synapses to be myelinated, i.e. the failure of synaptogenesis due to conditions such as insecure attachment, abuse, infection and trauma. There is also detailed information about the brains of children with Autism and conditions such as Tourette's Syndrome. It is suggested that you use this book to extend your knowledge of neuroscience but making reference to the learning of the babies and young children in your settings. Terms such as the 'listening brain', the 'visual brain', the 'searching brain' are used and research papers by other researchers have been included to provide examples of findings and to create opportunity for debate and analysis.

Gopnick, A; Meltzoff, A; Kuhl, P. (2001) *How Babies Think.* London: Phoenix (Orion Books Ltd)
This book was also published in the USA but the title used there was, '*The Scientist in the Nursery.*' When first published in the UK there was much discussion about the different titles. Some professionals thought that '*The Scientist in the Nursery*' painted a vivid picture

of the complexity of the brain and the way that babies learn. It offers food for thought, a text to dip in and out of. Chapter 5, '*What Scientists Have Learned About Children's Minds*', has strong links to this chapter.

Roberts, R; (2010) *Self-Esteem and Early Learning*, London: Sage
Chapter 1, '*Children Learning to be Lovable*', Provides an interesting comparison between old thinking and new thinking about the development of the brain. This supports the debates that have been included in this chapter about, perhaps, focusing too much on the sensitive periods for brain development or observing the baby or very young child and responding to their immediate needs.

References

Barlow, J (2016) Improving Relationships in the Perinatal Period: What Works in *AIMH UK Best Practice Guidance (BPG) No 1*, London: AIMH

Blair, C (2002) The On Track Guide – Section 1 https://www.beststart.org/OnTrack_English/pdf/OnTrack-Section1.pdf accessed December 2016

Blakemore, S J and Frith, U (2005) *The Learning Brain – lessons for education*, Oxford: Blackwell

Bowlby, J (1965) 2nd Ed *Child Care and the Growth of Love*, London: Penguin

Bowlby, J (1988/2005) *A Secure Base*, London: Routledge Classic

Carter, R (1998) *Mapping the Mind*, London: Weidenfeld & Nicholson (Orion Publishing Group Ltd)

Carter, R (2010) *Mapping the Mind*, London: Weidenfeld & Nicholson (Orion Books Ltd)

Corel, J L (1975) *The postnatal development of the human cerebral cortex*. Cambridge, MA: Harvard University Press; http://www.urbanchildinstitute.org/why-0-3/baby-and-brain accessed on line 31 December 2016

Gerhardt, S (2004) *Why Love Matters* East Sussex: Brunner-Routledge

Gopnick, A; Meltzoff, A and Kuhl, P. (2001) *How Babies Think*, London: Phoenix (Orion Books Ltd)

House, R (Ed.) (2011) *Too Much, Too Soon?* Gloucestershire: Hawthorn Press

Johnson, T (2016) Holistic Development: The Social and Emotional Needs of Children, in *The Early Years Handbook for Students and Practitioners*, I (Ed.) Trodd, L; Oxon: Routledge

Moss, P (2014) Transformative Change and Real Utopias in Early Childhood Education, Oxon: Routledge

Nolan, M (2016) 'The 21st Century Two Year Old: Ancient and Modern'. Presentation given at the SEFDEY National Meeting, March 2016

OECD/CERI (2007) *Understanding the Brain: The Birth of a Learning Science*, Paris: CERI – accessed 23 December 2016

Pally, R (2000) *The Mind-Brain Relationship*, London: Karnac Books

Reber, A S (1995) *The Penguin Dictionary of Psychology*, London: Penguin

Roberts, R (2010) *Self-Esteem and Early Learning*, London: Sage

Rose, J; Gilbert, L and Richards, V (2016) *Health and Wellbeing in Early Childhood*, London: Sage

Shore, R (1997) Rethinking the Brain: New Insights into Early Development, New York: Families and Work Institute

Siegal, D (2012) The Developing Mind: How Relationships and the Brain Interact to Shape Who We Are. New York: The Guilford Press.

Trevarthen, C (2002) Learning in Companionship in Education in the North in *The Journal of Scottish Education New Series*, No. 10, 2002 pp. 16–25

Trevarthen, C (July 2004) *Making Friends with Infants*, Paper presented at Pen Green Conference: Northampton.

Trevarthen, C (2011) What young children give to their learning, making education work to sustain a community and its culture in *'European Early Childhood Education Research Journal, The Journal of the European Early Childhood Education Research Association*, pp. 173–193 Oxon: Routledge, Taylor Francis Group

Websites

http://1.bp.blogspot.com/-xqrpQjqQiX8/T4GJukJ6grI/AAAAAAAABVU/mOeQ_6YVKNk/s1600/instinctual+brain.gif accessed 21 December 2016

http://www.learningdiscoveries.org/StagesofBrainDevelopment.html accessed 21 December 2016 Originated in Prentice Hall. Diagram of brain

http://www.who.int/about/mission/en/ accessed 31 December 2016

www.aimh.org.uk

www.sciencemediacentre.org/expert-reaction-to-the-biological-effects-of-day-care-as-published-in-the-biologist-a-journal-of-the-society-of-biology-2-

www.beginbeforebirth.org/for-schools/films#womb accessed 7 January 2017

www.who.int/about.definition/en/print.html

www.healthline.com>health>placenta accessed 12 January 2017

www.midwifery.org.uk accessed 12 January 2017

www.northumberlandlsgb.proceduresonline.com accessed 12 January 2017

2 Attachment theory

Key themes in this chapter

After reading this chapter you should be able to:

- Consider the evolution of attachment theory and the changes that may have occurred

- Identify, understand and discuss the different types of attachment

- Critique attachment theory

- Fully understand the importance of forming child to adult attachment

- Analyse the different types of attachment exhibited by children in your settings

- Relate attachment theory to Chapters 3, 4 and 5

- Consider adaptation of your policies related to children's transitions.

Introduction

This chapter commences with an exploration of the work on attachment by John Bowlby from 1956 onwards, his work with James and Joyce Robertson in the 1960s and subsequent research that has opposed or questioned some of these earlier theories and findings. Students and academics are encouraged to critique and analyse the different viewpoints and to consider the effects of secure and insecure attachments in relation to the development of strong neural pathways as presented in Chapter 1. The theory of attachment, the strange situation (Ainsworth), a secure base, different types of attachment such as secure attachment, ambivalent/resistant attachment, avoidant/insecure attachment and disorganised attachment and, the causes of the differing types are considered in some detail.

The reasons for inability to form strong attachments when, for example, a Mother has ill health, post-natal depression, substance abuse or has not experienced a secure attachment with her own Mother are included. There are links to the importance of sensitively managed transitions included in this chapter through discussions about and analysis of different situations, anecdotes and case studies. Reference is made to the chapters about Key Persons, Working with Parents and Carers and the Effects of Different Cultures and Cultural Experiences, where responses to the social and emotional needs and development of children are discussed. You are encouraged to reflect on the types of attachment thought to have been identified in the babies and young children attending your settings and how these findings might lead to changes in your responses to the babies, children and their parents or carers. International perspectives on attachment theory are introduced as further study in order to promote reflection on practice in the different childcare and educational settings internationally and in the United Kingdom.

Attachment

Bowlby explains the attachment of a baby or young child to their Mother or main carer as:

> Being strongly disposed to seek proximity to and contact with a specific figure and to do so in certain situations, notably when he is frightened, tired or ill . . . it is an attribute of the child and an attribute that gradually changes over time.

> (Bowlby 1991 p. 371)

Stern (1998) speaks about a child gaining 'senses of self', which develop when a child feels secure and attached to another responsive person with whom the child seeks to be in close proximity, with that person cuddling them, sharing their warmth and looking lovingly into the child's eyes, whilst Trevarthen (2002) speaks of attachment as *regulating the needs of one's own body*, asking for help and support from another person. In this instance he is comparing attachment with cultural learning which relates *one's own body to objects*.

Holmes (2001) identifies the characteristics of parents and carers who provide their baby and/or young children with secure attachment as demonstrating *attunement, sensitivity and responsiveness*, as also recognised by Mooney and

Munton (1997) and Barlow and Svanberg (2010) who included *warmth and synchrony*. Johnson (2016) considered the following factors that help to create a secure attachment between a Mother or main carer and a baby. When a baby is crying, he or she is communicating, signalling the fact that he or she is perhaps hungry, uncomfortable, hot, cold, afraid or feeling tired. The baby is seeking positive responses to its needs which, when received, help the child to feel safe and secure. This positive response that results in secure attachment also helps to regulate the levels of cortisol that are released when a baby or child is experiencing stress, as discussed in Chapter 1 in relation to the development of the brain.

Most Mothers respond to this by gazing at their baby whilst breast or bottle-feeding, thus making eye contact, using what nature has provided for the development of attachment bonds in that a baby's vision has a focal length of approximately 200 to 300 millimetres, allowing a feeding baby to focus on his or her Mother's face. The Mother will often speak about the way the baby may be feeling, whether they are sad, hungry or annoyed, using baby talk known as motherese, to help the baby realise that there is someone who understands his or her feelings, whilst gazing into the baby's eyes. The baby is beginning to gain a sense of self, as mentioned above, or a 'picture of themselves' from their Mother's 'loving acceptance' Dowling (2010). This is termed '*mirroring*' by Kohut, cited by Marrone (2000) due to the facial expressions of the Mother 'holding up a virtual mirror to the baby', Gerhardt (2004). The baby is beginning to know that he or she has the Mother's full attention and is also beginning to create an image of itself. This interaction is termed dyadic (Rutter 1993), between two people, in this case, the Mother and child. Barlow and Svanberg (2010) related research findings where Mothers who were able to interpret their baby's and young children's feelings, to predict play and language, had an ability for mind-mindedness. This mind-mindedness enabled the babies to 'represent thoughts and feelings through language and play, i.e. acquired representational system' (Barlow and Svanberg 2010 p. 5)

Humans are born with an innate desire to communicate and to be communicated with (Trevarthen 2009). Trevarthen also identified the musicality and rhythm during a proto-conversation between a Mother and baby which developed at two months of age, in that the vocal responses of the baby were of the same length and metre as the Mother's spoken phrases. If there is little response or a lack of positive response from the Mother, when the baby may be seeing a blank, depressed expression this begins to adversely affect the baby and over time affects the ability of the baby or very young child to form a secure attachment or relationships in later life. The baby tends to become disinterested and will gradually stop trying to communicate. Babies who have been experiencing negative responses have been observed to deliberately turn right away from a Mother's gaze despite the Mother, on occasions, endeavouring to gain the baby's attention. This is indicative of an insecure avoidant attachment in the baby in this instance.

The importance of secure attachment

The importance of a secure attachment was introduced in Chapter 1 in relation to the impact of insecure attachments on the development of the brain from conception and throughout childhood, particularly during the first three years of a child's life. Insecure attachments result in many of the neural pathways failing to connect. It is through the use of rapidly advancing technology such as MRI scans, used during research by neuroscientists, that the importance of the observational findings of researchers such as Freud, Bowlby, the Robertsons, Winnicott, Stern, Fonagy and Holmes, to name but a few, have been and are now being supported by substantive evidence. However, understanding emotional development and the complexity of secure and insecure attachments and separation anxiety is very difficult because, as identified by Bowlby, there are so many variables to each situation.

The importance of an attachment to a responsive adult was addressed by Sigmund Freud and Bowlby long before the findings of neuroscience. Bowlby acknowledged the fact that prior to his own research Freud had observed the importance of attachment and then separation anxiety which he saw as a 'key problem'. Freud was reported by Deigh (1991), when speaking about a child developing 'a conscience', as stating that 'children from birth to four years of age when helpless and completely dependent upon parents or carers form 'strong, loving attachments to their mothers'. Sigmund Freud also spoke about the fact that the child will not only see the parent as the person who provides care and nourishment but also as an authoritative person, thus moving ones' thoughts from initial attachment and dependence to future experiences in a child's life and independence (Deigh,1991 p. 298.)

Bowlby referred to observations made by Burlingham and Anna Freud on the reactions of children during separation from parents in the Second World War, in a wartime nursery. He identified similarities in their findings to his own. Marrone, for example

> intensified separation anxiety in later years', because, 'as a young child [he] had experienced mother as unreliable, or had periods of separation from her [and] is likely to become vulnerable to any subsequent sign of insecurity in the relationship.
>
> (Marrone 2000, p. 118)

Bowlby also referred to observations made by Spitz and Wolf (1946) in what would, perhaps have been termed, 'a home for unmarried mothers.' The children were cared for by their Mothers for the first few months and the environment did not change but after this time the Mothers were separated from their children for up to three months. (Bowlby 1991 pp. 24–25). Although these observations were detailed, a systematic method of recording was, apparently, not used. Bowlby was very systematic with his observations and research, which may be linked to the fact that he was 'qualified as a doctor, a psychiatrist, a psychoanalyst and a psychologist' (Bowlby 2005 p. xi).

Bowlby's research and theory of attachment have been recognised throughout the world. It began through his own research appointment with the World Health Organization (WHO) in 1950 in answer to a request by the United Nations to investigate the needs of homeless children (Bowlby 1988/2005). This research post resulted in Bowlby travelling to France, the Netherlands, Sweden, Switzerland, the United Kingdom and the United States of America, to gain an international perspective on the effects of homelessness (Bowlby 1965 p. 7). The report was presented to the United Nations in 1951. Marrone (2000) referred to Bowlby as the 'attachment theory creator.'

John Bowlby initially, during the 1950s, and like Winnicott above, spoke of Mother and child attachment, painting the picture of the Mother as the most important person in every child's life. Winnicott famously stated that

there is no such thing as an infant, only a mother and infant together.

(cited in Holmes 2001 p. 1)

Reflection I

Consider the statement above:

■ What is your immediate reaction?

■ What is the situation in today's culture?

■ How does this affect your own work with children?

■ Discuss this with colleagues.

This theme is returned to in Chapters 3 and 4.

It is important to note that during Bowlby's later research he changed his ideas because he identified the ability for a child to form a strong attachment to another significant adult, who did not have to be the Mother. It was recognised that the most important attribute of this significant other person was that they had to be able to be in tune with the needs of the baby. Bowlby, in his later papers, used the terminology of *'mother or permanent substitute mother'* (Bowlby 1965/1990).

Bowlby's research on attachment centred on the impact of a child's removal from its 'mother or permanent substitute mother.' There are three reasons why Bowlby chose to research the effects of 'the removal of a child from home to a residential nursery or hospital'

■ He believed it could have serious ill-effects on a child's personality development

■ There could be no debate as to whether it had occurred or not

■ It appeared to be a field in which preventative measures might be possible.

(Bowlby 1979 and 2005 p. 4)

These three reasons demonstrate that Bowlby was very aware that he should present substantive evidence to support his theory and that this would, ultimately, help to improve the lives of many children by identifying and responding to their emotional needs following bereavement, periods of separation and abuse.

The effects of separation

Bowlby's (1991) initial research was linked to the experiences of homeless children, as stated above, and children who had lost their Mothers. However, soon his focus became observing children who had been placed in residential children's homes or with foster carers for short stays of approximately two weeks' duration or had been hospitalised. The children were observed by James Robertson who, with his wife Joyce Robertson, also fostered children in their own home. The reasons for the children being placed in a residential home or with a foster carer were often linked to illness of the Mother or the birth of a new baby in the family. An example as shown in a video (watched by this author and used during teaching/lecturing between 1990 and 2006) and outlined below shows the effect of such a separation.

Case study I

Filmed by the Robertsons (1950s) accessed online 7 March 2017.

A small boy aged 17 months was placed in a residential home for nine days whilst his Mother was in hospital giving birth to his baby brother. The stages of separation anxiety that this child experienced were harrowingly obvious. At the beginning of the stay the child tried to communicate with the carers but his efforts were not responded to. He had no Key Worker, a subject that is further explored in detail in Chapter 3. The child displayed initial protest and anger in the form of crying, signs of loss, fear and anxiety and latterly depression when he sat in his cot and rocked backwards and forwards. Even though, initially, the child tried to communicate and befriend the nurses, there was a lack of reciprocation. The child initially exhibited a behaviour later described by Trevarthen as *'an innate desire to communicate'* (Trevarthen 2009). The father visited most evenings, but, gradually, as the child became depressed he did not interact with the father, he refused food at meal times and just sat. When his Mother arrived to collect him from the residential home to take him home with her, he rejected her, he would not allow her to hold and cuddle him. The website below provides a synopsis of the above vignette along with four other examples of children's reactions to separation.

http://www.robertsonfilms.info/young_children_in_brief_separation.htm

Bowlby (1988/2005) speaks about the impact these filmed observations have on the observer. The impact was and still is enormous. He mentions two films, *'a Peril in Infancy,'* filmed by Spitz, and *'A Two Year Old Goes to Hospital'*, filmed by James Robertson (1952). Analysis of the filmed observations drew the attention of professionals such as doctors, nurses and social workers to the effects of separation on very young children when admitted to hospital. These films, the analysis of the films and the resultant findings, very importantly resulted in changes to practice such as extended hospital visiting hours for children and parents being able to stay with children who are critically ill. It is observations such as these that demonstrate the anxiety experienced by very young children during periods of separation known as *'separation anxiety'* (Ainsworth in Bowlby 1969). However, it is also important to point out that although periods of separation do result in a child becoming anxious, if there is a strong attachment to the Mother or first carer, once the Mother or first carer returns the child will gradually settle and lose the feelings of anxiety. Whilst the importance of observation is being highlighted here, it is also very important that a child's past experiences are considered before analysing observations, or perhaps jumping to conclusions.

Reflection 2

Access the films mentioned above:

■ Choose one of the films to watch but consider the points about impact before watching it.

■ How did it make you feel?

(continued)

(continued)

- Have you yourself experienced a separation such as that observed?

- Did it bring back vivid memories of the experience or a time when you witnessed others experiencing separation?

- Do you think it has impacted on your later life or the later life of the person you witnessed?

- On remembering how you, or the person you witnessed, felt, how might you change your practice to ensure you support children more effectively?

Separation anxiety

Extreme levels of separation anxiety are very apparent in the above films and, as has already been stated, their impact resulted in changes in practice. However, at this stage, consider the effects of children attending childcare settings from seven or eight o'clock each morning until about six o'clock in the evening each weekday and, in some instances, overnight if parents or carers are working night shifts. Also, remember those children who experience multiple carers throughout each week. Johnson (2016) observed the fact that for babies between the ages of eight and ten months attending a childcare setting for the first time, the separation experience can prove to be very difficult. It is the time in a baby's life when they do not realise that if a person is not there, they still exist or, as Piaget and Inhelder (1969) identified, a baby has not yet developed the concept of object permanence. The babies also experience stranger danger at that time when the primary carer is not within their sight. Piaget developed a well- known, small experiment using an object and a blanket, hiding the object under the blanket. He found that by the age of nine to ten months the baby will begin to search for the hidden object. Thus, a baby is beginning to understand that people and objects exist even when they cannot be seen. It was found that once this concept was understood the babies generally settled more easily.

Although levels of separation anxiety can vary with the age of the child it is not just the age of the child that affects the levels of anxiety. They are certainly linked to prior experiences, their levels of resilience and the management of transitions, although, stating the obvious, good communication with all babies and children does help to alleviate the level of separation anxiety. Experience has confirmed the value of explaining to a child, of any age, what is going to happen to them, even a very tiny baby. Working with children of varying ages in many different settings, including a children's home, supported this belief. However, if we return to changes in practice within the health service, where the importance of the presence of the first carer was highlighted, should children today be spending such long hours in day care? Perhaps the issue of multiple carers should be taken into consideration in any setting, not only outside the child's home but within the child's home as illustrated in the following case study.

Case study 2

Milly is two years old and is usually cared for at home by family members, parents and, for three days each week, a nanny. She became very unsettled when the nanny was away for three weeks because she was unwell. Family members, with whom Milly is very 'close', provided the extra child care required by the working parents. She was and is very attached to her nanny and to her parents. The situation was explained to Milly by her Mother to prepare her for the fact that her nanny was going to be away and that different members of the family would be looking after her during the nanny's absence. Her daily routines were maintained throughout. Although Milly did not cry every day as her parents left, at times during the day the she would become very distressed, she did not want to go outside for walks or to play and exhibited changes in behaviours. For example, Milly did not like having her nappy changed. Even when the nappy was very dirty, she would cry and attempt to scratch and kick. The grandparents spoke to her gently and addressed the fact that she didn't like having her nappy changed by different people. Having acknowledged her feelings, as her nappy was changed, she stopped crying and kicking, relaxed completely and once the clean nappy was on, she sat up to cuddle the grandparent.

On return from work her Mother was greeted with smiles and cuddles each day. However, there were times when Milly did not respond to her parents either, possibly 'punishing them for leaving her with different carers. Milly is a child who is generally relatively placid, is sociable, eager to play, to communicate and to be out and about. Her reaction to the changes was very apparent, it may well have been separation anxiety. The situation was discussed with her parents in an endeavour to minimise her anxiety and to ensure that her routine was maintained and her behaviours were managed in a consistent way. Transitions between one carer and the next were managed with sensitivity in that grandparents stayed overnight before providing care so that there was no sudden transition. When her parents returned home the grandparents remained to help and to ensure another smooth transition. However, one should remember that parents return home from work feeling tired, at a time that is close to the child's bath-time and bedtime, when the child is obviously tired too. Therefore, there were many aspects within this situation to consider. Once the nanny returned to provide care, Milly became settled again.

Discuss the case study and consider the following question:

Whilst the issue in this case study has been identified as separation anxiety, was this the only reason for the behaviours or could there have been other aspects that should be explored?

Milly is a child from what one would describe as a happy, loving, respectful environment. However, she was observed to exhibit behaviours which could be identified as the phases of separation anxiety in that she cried and attempted to scratch and kick because she was feeling a sense of loss of the people to whom she was primarily attached and exhibiting signs of self-protection. She was possibly worried about the nanny who, she had been told, was ill and in hospital. A sense of loss is a part of attachment felt by the young child when in a situation like Milly's or when a child attends a childminder, day care or a nursery for the first few times and is separated from their primary carer. At no time did the carers think that Milly was just being 'difficult' or 'playing up'; they understood the reasons why she was upset and verbalised her feelings, which did help her to relax and feel reassured, as observed in her expression, her body moving from being tense to relaxed and then wanting a hug and to play again. The grandparents held the needs of Milly in mind and showed the capacity for mind-mindedness Barlow and Svanberg (2009) because they were able to interpret her actions and feelings and respond appropriately by talking to Milly about how she was possibly feeling.

Some of the points in this case study are returned to in Chapters 3 and 4 when considering the role of the Key Worker and the importance of working in partnership with parents. The strength of attachment depends upon many factors of life, especially early experiences, and, as has been illustrated here, the point of time in the life of the child. It helps to illustrate the vital role that all Early Years' Practitioners have when working with very young and vulnerable children. Bowlby (1969), Ainsworth (1978), Shore (2001) and Gerhardt (2004) have all identified the fact that secure attachments are vital in reducing the levels of anxiety. Refer back to Chapter 1 for the prolonged effects of stress and anxiety on the development of the brain caused by raised cortisol levels.

There are several levels of anxiety; they are dependent upon the prior experiences children have been exposed to, for example separation anxiety for older children if they have been placed in care with a foster carer. A strong attachment may have developed between the foster carer and the child which may lead to feelings of conflict for the child because they still have a sense of attachment and loyalty towards their Mother. It is important, at this point, to consider the reasons why a child might be with a foster carer. The child may have been placed because a parent had to be hospitalised, when the placement is for a short period of time, or it may be because the child has been placed by Social Services because there have been parenting concerns or there is evidence of poor parenting. It was identified by Anna Freud that children will still cling to their parents, even when the parent/s 'are hostile and sometimes cruel to them', (cited by Marrone 2000 p. 118). Therefore, one should, as stated above, always take into consideration the prior experiences of the child and their family.

When identifying the presence of separation anxiety, it is important to consider, as well as prior experiences, the age and the stage of the child. It is appropriate for a very young child to cry, scream, kick, scratch, show signs of anger and then become quiet and withdrawn. However, an older child will not usually react in this way when their Mother or carer departs but they may become quiet and withdrawn, hiding their feelings of fear, loss and anxiety. The older child may have developed ways of coping with separation or may have a high level of resilience that enables them to adapt to their new situations. Always be aware of changes in behaviour and consider the causes. Try not to jump to conclusions. This topic is considered in Chapters 3 and 4.

Separation and loss is experienced in many different forms throughout life, not just when separated from a parent or first carer. The signs and symptoms of separation anxiety are very similar to those experienced following a bereavement, namely protest, anger and loss. Children can also be seen protesting and being very angry when their favourite toy is snatched away, this is a small example of loss, but, it could be the child's favourite toy or their transitional object (Winnicott 1971/2005 in Johnson 2016), the very thing that helps a child adapt to a new setting, their important link to home and their Mother or first carer.

Separation anxiety has been identified in the films discussed earlier in this chapter and in the case studies. It was from observations such as these that the different types of attachment were identified by Mary Ainsworth and the Strange Situation Assessment was developed.

Types of attachment

Many of you will know that Mary Ainsworth created an observation tool to record infants' reaction to strange situations, known as the Strange Situation Assessment. This assessment tool was developed to determine whether the child was securely or insecurely attached to the Mother. The reactions of the child were recorded during play with the Mother and with a stranger, as the Mother left the room, throughout the period of separation and as the Mother returned to the room. During the second phase of the assessment the Mother leaves the room, the child is alone, the stranger enters and responds to the child, the Mother re-enters. The whole sequence lasted approximately 20 minutes.

This sequence can be accessed via the following website:

http://www.childdevelopmentmedia.com/articles/mary-ainsworth-and-attachment-theory/ accessed 5 March 2017

Once you have accessed the video, consider and discuss the way that the sessions are set up and consider your thoughts as you observed the infants being assessed. Do you think that realistic results have been achieved? Barlow and Svanberg (2010) described this assessment as reliable and valid, 'the gold standard in the assessment of an infant's attachment behaviour' (Barlow and Svanberg 2010 p. 100).

It is with the Strange Situation Assessment that Ainsworth was enabled to identify and assess three types of attachment:

Secure Attachment which is identified when a child is seen to explore and play in a new environment whilst the Mother is present, will engage with the stranger, cry as the Mother leaves the room and be comforted by the Mother on their return but will not interact with a stranger in the presence of the Mother, although he or she may smile from a distance.

Anxious Ambivalent Insecure Attachment is identified when a child does not explore and play in a new environment, cries bitterly when the Mother leaves but is ambivalent on her return, remains close but resents her efforts to provide comfort. This is also termed resistant attachment, as explained by Gerhardt (2004).

Anxious Avoidant Insecure Attachment is identified when a child does not show interest in the environment and does not react when the Mother leaves the room or when she returns and reacts in a similar way with the stranger. There is a general lack of emotion displayed.

Different levels of resistant and avoidant attachment have been identified during research within different cultures in the United States, North and South Germany and Japan, as cited by Stern (1998). Findings were:

- resistant or avoidant attachment in 12 and 20 percent of US middleclass samples

- South German samples reflected US norms

- North German samples showed avoidant attachment

- Japanese children showed resistant attachment.

(Stern 1998 pp. 187–188)

Whilst Stern considered different methods of research, should consideration also have been given to the different cultural approaches to parenting and life in general?

Holmes (2001) identified six domains of attachment theory in relation to the setting where he worked as a psychotherapist:

1. Secure base – without which survival is impossible

2. Exploration and enjoyment

3. Protest and anger

4. Loss

5. Internal working models – are the way in which the child/adult builds up representations of relationships and base expectations of current interpersonal interactions on past experiences

(Bowlby 1988 in Holmes 2001, Johnson 2016)

Internal working models are also explained as:

developing significant neural connections within the brain, forming a basis for effective stress regulation.

(Rose, Gilbert, and Richards 2016 p. 56)

6. Reflexive function and narrative competence – the ability to be able to talk about oneself and difficult situations.

You might consider these six domains of attachment in relation to the different types of attachment observed in your childcare settings. They may assist your analysis of the observations you have made in relation to the area of learning for personal, social and emotional development as well as attachment and loss. You should be enabled to interpret and analyse the findings from your observations of the children, such as the children's types of attachment being observed, the level of separation anxiety, the children's ability to adapt to the setting and their Key Person and their ability to explore and enjoy their play. Domains 5 and 6 may be discussed when considering the requirements of the DfES (2008); DfE 2012; 2017) for example:

are children able to manage their social behaviours and to speak about feelings and develop a sense of empathy?

They may provide a helpful tool when observing children who you have identified as possibly exhibiting insecure attachment to their first carer. These points are further discussed below and in more detail in Chapters 3 and 4. Domain 5, internal working models, may also be considered in relation to learned patterns of behaviour, for example 'responds to my cry', 'picks me up', 'coat being put on' relates to going out, as recorded by Gerhardt (2004). These are also termed, 'representations of interactions', by Stern (1998); 'emotional Schemas', by Bucci (1997) and, 'procedural memory', by Clymen (1991). (Gerhardt 2004: p. 24)

Reflection 3

Think about the six domains:

■ What is your definition of a secure base?

■ Does your setting provide a secure base?

■ How do you welcome children and parents into your setting?

■ Do you observe new children exploring and enjoying being in the setting and playing with the toys?

■ Do you observe children exhibiting the emotions of protest and anger when their parent/carer leaves?

■ Do you observe children exhibiting resistant/ambivalent behaviours when their parent/carer returns to your setting?

Before exploring a secure base in more detail think about Holmes' suggestion that Bowlby sometimes implied 'that all that was needed for a secure attachment to develop was a secure base'; this was in relation to a psychotherapeutic situation. Are these terms interdependent? Is this all that we need to provide in our childcare settings?

A secure base

When thinking about a secure base one could consider the environment alone. However, is this what is meant by a secure base? In terms of attachment a secure base is very strongly linked to the early relationships between a baby and the first carer, who may not necessarily be the Mother. It is the Mother's or carer's ability to provide basic needs of food and warmth along with empathy, acknowledgement and appropriate, sensitive responses to the ever-changing needs of the baby that helps to create this secure base. Consideration should be given as to whether the Mother or carer is able to develop the concept of 'mirroring' as described in the paragraph on attachment. Rose et al. (2016, referring to Siegel and Bryson 2011) developed 'a framework of 4 S's of attachment', Seen, Safe, Soothed and Secure, the secure base that is innately being searched for by the baby. Thus, the presence of the Mother or carer, providing consistency and appropriate reciprocal responses to the needs of the baby or very young child is essential.

Fonagy (2003) explored the concept of attachment linked to the genetic system of each child, that is parenting versus genetics – what role does a parent take in the social development of the child? He acknowledged the importance of attachment to the first carer and the effects on future development should strong attachments not be formed within the early years. However, he suggested that the process is very complex and that the genetics of the child may influence the response of the adult to the child's behaviours. He explored the fact that there may be a connection between attachment, the Internal Working Model, developing a sense of self (introduced above), and the Interpersonal Interpretative Mechanism (developing awareness of others) within the child. This may also be influenced by the Mother's own attachment model (Crittenden 2004, cited in Barlow and Svanberg 2010). It would appear that Bowlby's analysis of the complexity and many variables within each situation when assessing the levels of attachment, whether it be secure or insecure, are being proven through continuing research and advances in technology.

The focus of this chapter has been on attachment between baby and Mother or first carer. It has been recognised for decades that children are able to form attachments to more than one adult or Mother figure. Stern (1998) has spoken about attachments changing and developing throughout life, so that attachments do not remain static. These 'selective attachments' (Rutter and Rutter 1993) begin to occur between the ages of one and three years and continue throughout life.

Reflection 4

- Consider the different forms of attachment that you yourself have experienced.

- List them in order of importance to you

- Ask yourself why they were important

- How did you feel when some of the attachments changed?

- What events may cause changes in attachment levels?

Attachment to secondary care givers is considered specifically and in detail in Chapter 3 when the role of the Key Person is addressed, including the management of separation anxiety, insecure attachments and the impact that these situations can have, not only on the child but also on the Key Person. The emotional needs of babies and very young children have been included in the content of the Early Years Foundation Stage (EYFS) since 2008, this has resulted in the inclusion of statements such as 'must ensure support for children's emotional well-being to help them to know themselves' (DfFS 2008 p. 12). It is one of the three prime areas of learning, 'personal, social and emotional development', in the DfE 2012 and is, thankfully, still included in the most recent EYFS Statutory Framework (DfE 2017).

It is statutory for each child to be allocated a 'Key Person'.

(EYFS 2017)

However, it could be argued that this offers insufficient emphasis on 'emotional needs' and the 'Key Person'. The focus of this book is the 'emotional needs' of each child as opposed to the 'emotional development' of each child whereas the EYFS focuses on personal, social and emotional development. Are we able to ensure the personal, social and emotional development of each child if the key adults do not observe, recognise and respond to an emotional need with empathy and understanding? Responding is practicing the 4 S's of attachment, being *Seen, Safe, Soothed and Secure*, Rose et al. (2016). If insecure attachment is observed and identified, the reasons for the insecure attachment must be considered.

The causes of insecure attachments

The causes and impacts of insecure attachments were introduced in Chapter 1 in relation to the development of the brain and forming of neural connections. The subject is revisited here focusing specifically on the health and wellbeing of the Mother during the antenatal and postnatal periods and the effect this might have on the ability to form secure attachments. Chronic physical conditions of the Mother that can impact on the health of the baby include diabetes, and cardiac and pulmonary disease, three conditions which may be exacerbated by pregnancy. However, there are many other conditions that may be considered, but it is not necessarily these conditions themselves that affect the baby because they can be due to the medication the Mother has been prescribed. Diabetes can affect the foetus and newborn baby who must be monitored regularly during the first days of life, especially the for their blood sugar levels. Whilst these physical conditions do not affect the ability to form secure attachments, there is the possibility that chronic illness can impact on the mental health of the Mother which may result in an insecure attachment between Mother and baby.

This may be especially so during a pregnancy when the Mother maybe concerned not just for her own health but also the health of her baby. It has now been suggested that a stressed Mother during pregnancy can result in an anxious baby (Barlow 2016); the First 1001 days (2016). Most Mothers, during their pregnancy, begin to form attachments with their baby, especially once the baby's movements have been felt. They talk to their baby and stroke their abdomen when sitting relaxed. However, if the Mother is unable to progress through pregnancy relating to her baby and forming a maternal-foetal attachment, the possible consequence is that she will be unable to form an attachment with her newborn infant. Gerhardt (2004) includes a Mother's *relationship with their feelings* as another of the reasons a Mother may not be able to form a secure attachment. Forming a *good relationship* is the result of being able to interpret ones' own feelings as well as interpreting those of a baby, young child or other adult.

Provocation I

A three year-old child attends your setting. The Mother had a new baby approximately three weeks ago. The three year-old has continued to attend the setting and appears happy whilst there. You notice that the Mother appears very tired, uncommunicative and distant. When you ask how she is and pass a comment saying how lovely the new baby is, she does not respond. You try to enquire, gently if all is well, she just shrugs her shoulders. You invite her to have a cup of tea or coffee which is refused. You ask if she has seen the Health Visitor of her GP because she appears tired. She leaves the setting without responding.

Who would you share your concerns with and who might you contact outside the setting? Given that the baby is only three weeks old, you might telephone the Health Visitor to see if they would visit Mother and baby. A situation such as this will not only impact on the attachment between the new baby and the Mother but will also not help the older child who may already be a little unhappy about having a new brother or sister. When the Mother returns to collect the older child, you may find that she is more communicative and suggest she phones the Health Visitor herself or enquire if she has family nearby who may be able to help. It is important for you to offer support to the parents and carers who attend your setting, as discussed in Chapter 4. The Mother in this provocation might be very tired but there is the possibility that she is showing signs of postnatal depression.

The Peer Early Education Partnership (PEEP) which commenced in 1995 in Oxford was developed to support parents, in many ways to enable parents to learn together, in groups and with their babies and very young children. It gave parents confidence by recognising them as their baby's or very young child's first educator; it enhanced the relationships between parents and young children through music and singing and through talking, reading to their babies and young children and sharing books. Evaluation of the PEEP project found the PEEP Mothers:

■ Reported taking more basic skills courses

■ Significantly improved their socioeconomic status

■ Reported significantly greater awareness of their child's literacy development and ways to foster it through modelling skills, play and music

■ Developed more occupation-related skills

■ Reported more understanding of their child's general development.

(Barlow and Svanberg 2010 p. 95)

A marvellous quote that supports the evaluation, made by one of the Mothers illustrates the impact that initiatives such as PEEP can have on life and lives of parents and children:

> l learned children have lots of abilities and if we give them opportunities to explore . . . go out and talk about things . . . they are not just a plant that we water. We have to give them opportunity. I learned how to play, touch and feel and enjoy being with my child. I learned the importance of music and song. I learned confidence that I could cope with the early months and child behaviour.
>
> (Roberts 2001 cited in Barlow and Svanberg 2010 p. 89)

Trevarthen (2009) also highlighted the importance of interactions between Mothers and tiny babies, dyadic interactions (interaction between two people) in the form of song and conversation which, as mentioned earlier in the chapter, are imperative in helping to develop secure attachments.

The inability for a child to form a secure attachment within the first 1001 days has been shown to have a profound effect on ability to form secure attachments throughout his or her life. It has also been proven to affect, not only a child's social and emotional development and their ability to form relationships but their all-round development and prospects throughout life. The impact on the Mother's health and wellbeing, with the possible consequences for the baby, should the Mother not form a strong attachment is now being fully recognised by Government following the publication of a Cross Party Manifesto.

A Cross Party Manifesto, first issued in 2013 and updated in 2016, supports the importance of the first 1001 days of a child's life from conception to two years of age. It highlights this time, as identified in Chapter 1, as a very important time for the development of the brain – creating strong neural pathways.

> the earliest experiences shape the development of the brain and have a life-long effect on a baby's mental and emotional health.'
>
> The child's response to experiences of fear or tension have been set to danger and high alert. This will also occur at any time during the first 1001 days when exposed to overwhelming stress from any cause within the family, such as parental mental illness, maltreatment or exposure to domestic violence.
>
> A baby's social and emotional development is affected by their attachment to their parents.
>
> (The 1001 Critical Days 2016 p. 5)

The manifesto has a range of far reaching visions that would help to improve experiences for babies during the first 1001 critical days, mainly through working closely with parents during the antenatal and postnatal periods. Two of the visions that directly relate to Early Years Practitioners in the manifesto are that:

> The health and early years' workforce should receive high quality training in infant mental health and attachment as standard.
>
> Childminders, nurseries and childcare settings caring for under 2s must focus on the attachment needs of babies and infants, with Ofsted providing specific guidance on how this can be measured effectively.
>
> (The 1001 Critical Days 2016 p. 9)

There is a total of thirteen points within the vision which includes other areas such as:

- identifying vulnerable families, encouraging parent/infant interactions

- employing specialist midwives and health visitors trained in parent and infant mental health

- encouraging parents to attend antenatal classes which include all aspects of parenting including health and welfare and social and emotional development

- working in close partnership with other professionals to support the parents and infants, including access to Consultant Perinatal Psychiatrists if necessary

- Children's Centres are to provide universal services primarily to those most in need and opportunities to register the birth of a baby at the centres.

Conclusion

The importance of secure attachment and the results of insecure attachment which have been explored in this chapter cannot be overemphasised. John Bowlby, as identified through the research for this chapter, has always been cited as the person who initially influenced our practice today. He identified the need for each child to be given the opportunity to form a secure attachment with their first carer. The first carer should have the ability to demonstrate a sensitive responsiveness (Barlow and Svanberg 2010) and be attuned to the infant's needs (Holmes 2001). Bowlby's theory was questioned by some researchers prior to research by neuroscientists during the 1990s. The results obtained using modern technology to scan the brain substantiated the need for each baby and young child to form a secure attachment with a significant adult, the Mother or first carer. The main point that has been woven throughout the chapter is the importance of the adult's responses to the emotional needs of a baby or young child in enabling progression and development throughout his or her life.

You have been encouraged to reflect on and analyse case studies and to relate your reflections to practice in your own Early Years settings. Through these reflections you should be able to implement changes that may improve the responses of Practitioners to the emotional needs of the children in your care. The chapter has reaffirmed the role of the Key Person and the resultant, important responsibilities a Key Person has. It is recommended that you read or refer to the following texts and to related texts in the Reference list to expand and deepen your knowledge about attachment theory still further. This will enable you to analyse and discuss the emotional needs of the children attending your settings. Your role as a Key Person has also been referenced in relation to the requirements of the EYFS and Government policy. The requirements of the EYFS and Government policy are areas that will always fuel debate but your role as a Key Person is vital in relation to the emotional needs of very young children. As discussed throughout this chapter the importance of secure attachments and the effects of insecure attachments continue to be paramount and, therefore, should be kept in mind by you and reflected upon. This theme is explored in detail in Chapter 3 where the impact of attachment on the Key Person and implications for practice are considered in more detail.

Further reading

The 1001 Critical Days Cross-Party Manifesto 2016

It is suggested that you read this manifesto in full and then critique the content considering the current climate of change, for example reducing Local Authority funding, the resultant closure of many Children's Centres especially in rural areas, and the impact of the free 30 hours on Private and Voluntary settings. The importance of the concept of working in close collaboration with other relevant professionals cannot be emphasised enough. It is vital, if this vision is to be achieved and children's mental health and emotional needs are to be met. One could put forward a very, very strong case for the growing importance of the Early Years Workforce where the emotional needs of very young children are first identified and first referrals to other professionals are made. It is vitally important that the voice of the Early Years Workforce is heard, listened to, respected and acted upon because Early Years Practitioners and Key Persons are often the first to identify the emotional and developmental needs of a very young child. The Cross-Party Manifesto does include recommendations for each area to have a Children's Centre and the importance of having a well - qualified Early Years Workforce with knowledge of the emotional needs of baby's and young children, their health and well-being.

Barlow, J; Svanberg, P O (2010) *Keeping the Baby in Mind Infant Mental Health Practice,* Routledge: East Sussex.

A very interesting text that will provide you with in-depth knowledge about working with parents, especially those requiring extra support. Topics directly related to those introduced and discussed in this chapter include:

- *Keeping the baby in mind*

- *Promoting the early parent-infant relationship*

- *Promoting a secure attachment*

- *Developing infant-centred services.*

A further chapter expands the information on the Peers Early Education Partnership (PEEP) you have already read about in this chapter, 'Keeping the baby in mind' is Empowering parents through – 'Learning together'. This chapter explains that the aim of the programme was 'to begin to work with babies and their families', in order to 'improve the educational attainment of the whole community'(Barlow and Svanberg 2010 pp. 89–90).

Although it appears that this text relates to working with parents, the significance here is linked to the formation of secure attachments through early, appropriate, sensitive interactions between first carers, usually Mothers and their babies.

Rose, J; Gilbert, L; Richards, V (2016) *Health and Well-being in Early Childhood*, London: Sage.

Throughout this book there are references to the importance of attachment to a significant first carer and subsequent attachments to Key Persons for babies and very young children. Chapter 5 *Attachments and Early Relationships*, and Chapter 6 *Emotional Development and Regulation* provide helpful links to the theories of attachment and emotional development, as the titles suggest. They support discussions introduced in this chapter and ideas on the development of the brain and the important role of the Key Person.

Ziv, Y; Kaplan, B. A; Venza, J (2015) Practicing attachment in the real world: improving maternal insightfulness and dyadic emotional availability at an outpatient community, mental health clinic, in *Attachment & Human Development* June 2016 Vol. 18, No. 3 2016 pp. 292–313, UK: Routledge.

This study was undertaken because until this time most 'attachment based intervention programmes' had been conducted within university partnerships. It took place in a mental health clinic because the researchers wished to monitor the effects of the intervention programmes in the 'real world, i.e in real life settings' where the intervention often continued for many years as opposed to short interventions of six to nine months. It is suggested that you compare this research with intervention programmes in the UK, especially in relation to the length of the intervention.

Pace, U; Zappulla, C; Di Maggio, R (2016) The mediating role of perceived peer support in the relation between quality of attachment and internalising problems in adolescence: a longitudinal perspective in *Attachment & Human Development* October 2016 Vol. 18, No.5 pp. 508–525, UK: Routledge.

The research for this article was based in Italy. It has been chosen because it provides an international perspective. It is a longitudinal study that explores, as the title implies, the impact the different levels of attachment experienced during the early years have on forming attachments and relationships, social expectations, self-esteem and ability to internalise problems during adolescence.

References

Ainsworth, M, Blehar, M, Waters, E and Wall, S (1978) *Patterns of Attachment*. Hillsdale, NJ: Earlbaum

Barlow, J (2016) Improving Relationships in the Perinatal Period: What Works, in *AIMH UK Best Practice Guidance (BPG) No 1*, London: AIMH

Barlow, J; Svanberg, P O (2010) *Keeping the Baby in Mind: Infant Mental Health Practice*, Routledge: East Sussex

Blakemore, S J; Frith, U (2005) *The Learning Brain – lessons for education*, Oxford: Blackwell

Bowlby, J (1965/1990) 2nd Ed *Child Care and the Growth of Love*, London: Penguin

Bowlby, J (1969/1991) 2nd Ed *Attachment and Loss: Volume1, Attachment*, London: Penguin

Bowlby, J (1988/2005) *A Secure Base*, London: Routledge Classic

Bowlby, J (2005) The Making and Breaking of Affectional Bonds, Oxon: Routledge Classics

Bucci, W (1997) *Psychoanalysis and Cognitive Science: A multiple code theory*. NY: Guilford Press

Clyman, R B (1991) The Procedural Organization Of Emotions: A Contribution From Cognitive Science To The Psychoanalytic Theory Of Therapeutic Action in, *The Journal of the American Psychoanalytic Association*, pp. 349–382 https://www.scribd.com/document/172340247/Clyman-R-Procedural-Organization-of-Emotions-Affect-Psychoa-Perspectives-p-349-38219921 accessed 16 February 2018

Deigh, J (1991) Freud's Later Theory of Civilization in *The Cambridge Companion to Freud*, Cambridge: Cambridge University Press

DfE (2012) The Statutory Framework for the Early Years Foundation Stage, Runcorn: DfE accessed on line March 2014

DfE (2014) The Statutory Framework for the Early Years Foundation Stage, Runcorn: DfE accessed on line March 2014

DfE (2017) The Statutory Framework for the Early Years Foundation Stage, Runcorn: DfE accessed on line March 2017

DfES (2008) *The Early Years Foundation Stage*, London: DfES Publications

Dowling, M (2010) 3rd Ed Young Children's Personal, Social and Emotional Development London: Paul Chapman

Fonagy, P (2003) The development of psychopathology from infancy to adulthood: the mysterious unfolding of disturbance in time', in *Infant Mental Health Journal*, 24 (3): 212–239. May 2003, accessed on line – 10 April 2017

Gerhardt, S (2004) *Why Love Matters*, East Sussex: Brunner-Routledge

HMSO Cross Party Manifesto (2013) – *The 1001 Critical Days*: HMSO

HMSO Cross Party Manifesto (2016) – *The 1001 Critical Days*: HMSO

Holmes, J (2001) *The Search for the Secure Base*, East Sussex: Brunner-Routledge

Johnson, T (2016) Holistic Development: The Social and Emotional Needs of Children, in *The Early Years Handbook for Students and Practitioners*, Ed Trodd, L; Oxon: Routledge

Marrone, M (2000) *Attachment and Interaction*, London: Jessica Kingsley Publications

Mooney, A and Munton, A G (1997) *Research and Policy in Early Childhood Services: Time for a New Agenda*. London: Institute of Education, University of London

Pace, U; Zappulla, C; Di Maggio, R (2016) The mediating role of perceived peer support in the relation between quality of attachment and internalising problems in adolescence: a longitudinal perspective, in *Attachment & Human Development 2016* Vol. 18, No. 5 pp. 508–525, UK: Routledge

Piaget, J; Inhelder, B (1969) *The Psychology of the Child*, USA: Basic Books Inc

Rose, J; Gilbert, L; Richards, V (2016) *Health and Well-being in Early Childhood*, London: Sage

Rutter, M; Rutter, M (1993) *Developing Minds* London: Penguin The New Early Years www.sciencemediacentre.org/expert-reaction-to-the-biological-effects-of-day-care-as-published-in-the-biologist-a-journal-of-the-society-of-biology-2-2/ accessed 27 April 2014

Shore, R (2001) 'Effects of a secure attachment relationship on right brain development, affect regulation and infant mental health', *Infant Mental Health Journal*, 22 (1–2), pp. 7–66

Stern, D N (1998) *The Interpersonal World of the Infant*, London: Karnac Books

Trevarthen, C (2002) Learning in Companionship in Education in the North: *The Journal of Scottish Education New Series*, No. 10, 2002 pp. 16–25

Trevarthen, C (2009) Why Attachment Matters in *Sharing Meaning HUMAN NEEDS & HUMAN SENSE: THE NATURAL SCIENCE OF MEANING* file:///G:/Book%20-%20Emotional%20Needs/Colwyn-Trevarthen-2009-Human-Needs-and-Human-Sense.pdf accessed online March 2017

Winnicott, D W (1971) *Playing and Reality*, (2005 edition, Routledge Classics) Oxon: Routledge C

Websites

http://1.bp.blogspot.com/-xqrpQjqQiX8/T4GJukJ6grI/AAAAAAAABVU/mOeQ_6YVKNk/s1600/instinctual+brain.gif accessed 21 December 2016

http://www.1001criticaldays.co.uk/news-press-releases/1001-critical-days-conception-age-two accessed 8 December 2017

http://www.childdevelopmentmedia.com/articles/mary-ainsworth-and-attachment-theory/ accessed 5 March 2017

http://www.learningdiscoveries.org/StagesofBrainDevelopment.html accessed 21 December 2016

http://www.robertsonfilms.info/young_children_in_brief_separation.htm

www.aimh.org.uk

www.beginbeforebirth.org/for-schools/films#womb accessed 7 January 2017

www.education.gov.uk/publications

www.healthline.com>health>placenta accessed 12 January 2017

www.legislation.gov.uk/

www.midwifery.org.uk accessed 12 January 2017

www.northumberlandlsgb.proceduresonline.com accessed 12 January 2017

www.sciencemediacentre.org/expert-reaction-to-the-biological-effects-of-day-care-as-
   published-in-the-biologist-a-journal-of-the-society-of-biology-2-

www.uni.edu/universitas/archive/fall06/pdf/art_praglin.pdf

www.who.int/about.definition/en/print.html

www.webarchives.gov.uk

3 Key Persons

Adults' responses to children

Key themes in this chapter

After reading this chapter you should be able to:

■ Analyse and critique the way in which different Early Years settings encompass the Key Person Approach

■ Articulate the importance of a Key Person for each child in an Early Years Setting

■ Consider your role as a Key Person

■ Analyse your role as a Key Person

■ Reflect on and analyse the planning and provision for your key children

■ Appreciate the difficulties that may be experienced by a Key Person

■ Consider the importance of ensuring support and supervision for staff in relation to their role as a Key Person.

Introduction

As a Key Person, it is vital that you expand your knowledge and thoughts on attachment theory, the requirement for a secure base for children and the ability of children to become attached to more than one significant person. Initially this chapter includes the historic development/evolution of the Key Person Approach from Bowlby's research through to its implementation when it became mandatory in 2008. It interrelates with and encourages you to refer to Chapters 1, 2 and 4 where references to the importance of a Key Person are introduced in relation to neuroscience, attachment theory and working with parents. Consideration is given to the importance of a calm, welcoming, secure environment where a sense of warmth provided by the Key Persons is evident and where the play and related learning reflect the needs and interests of the children. You are encouraged to reflect on the links between theory and practice within your own Early Years settings when planning and providing for the needs of each of your key children in relation to the in-depth observations you have recorded, particularly in relation to the children's emotional needs and emotional well-being. This enables you to reflect on and to analyse the impact of your Key Person role upon the children and their parents. At the end of the chapter, it explores, in some detail, the impact of being a Key Person on each member of staff, both the advantages and difficulties as well as the support that may be required for each Key Person.

A historic perspective and development of the Key Person approach within Early Years

Bowlby identified the ability for children to form attachments to more than one significant person during his research in the 1950s and 1960s, as discussed in Chapter 2, where the importance of a baby/child being able to relate to and form an attachment to a significant person, their Mother or Carer has been highlighted. Research from the 1970s and up to the present day, into the effects of experiences in day care on very young children's emotional development and well-being, has resulted in the implementation of the Key Person Approach. The title Key Person Approach (Elfer et al. 2003) rather than Key Person system has been adopted here because it is thought to be less formal or clinical and more in keeping with childcare and education. Elfer et al chose this title because, 'it is so much about human relationships . . . it is about very young children's relationships with adults' (Elfer et al. 2003 p. 31).

Goldschmied and Jackson (2004) cite Bain and Barnett (1980) who found that each child was being handled by several different members of staff, and Marshall (1982) who found that children were not experiencing the one to one, adult/child interaction so necessary to enable very young children to settle and have their individual needs met. Hay (1997) speaks of the 'Key Worker' being a 'special person to whom to relate' and 'providing a dependable relationship to ease times of transition at the beginning and end of the day.' The term special person begins to paint the picture of someone who is relating well and forming a special bond with their key children. Perhaps the second part of the quote about transitions at the beginning and end of the day could be interpreted in such a way as to imply that this is the only time available for these special relationships and this could be aligned with the concerns expressed by other researchers. Elfer et al. (2003)

and Goldschmied and Jackson (2004) who found that Key Workers did not always provide all the care and education needed by their key children, 'Other members of staff were observed feeding and changing the very young children.' Thus, the special relationships/attachment bonds, one would expect to observe, were not always being formed with the Key Worker/Key Person.

Points to consider:

- Could this initially be considered as 'tokenism' in that members of staff were being allocated a number of children who would be their Key Children but in name only?

- Or could it have been due to the fact that the Key Worker System/Approach was new to Early Years Practitioners who did not perhaps understand the full concept of the requirements of a Key Person?

Whilst most children are able to form an attachment to more than one person those persons have to be interested in, to be able to interact with and form close relationship with the child/children, as identified by Davison (2013), Goldschmied and Jackson (2004), Elfer et al (2003), Gerhardt (2004) and Manning-Morton (2006). Despite the research, papers and books addressing these issues, the experiences for many very young children have been and still are reported as lacking.

Provocation 1

Davison (2013) presents a case study which includes an incident where a parent observed members of staff in the baby room talking together in a corner whilst the babies were left in their cots, many of them crying. It was reported that the members of staff made no attempt to pick the babies up to comfort them. The staff explained that this was because it was a 'quiet time' for the babies.

(Davison 2013 p. 43)

Consider your initial reaction to this example.

- How does it make you feel?

- Have you observed a situation such as this in any setting where you have worked?

- How was the situation managed?

- What should have been happening?

It is evident here, from the publication date, that this case study was shared after the implementation of Birth to Three Matters (2002) and the EYFS (DfES 2008) when one would have hoped each baby had been allocated a Key Person, who, despite the routine of the nursery, would have been responding to the baby's needs, providing cuddles, comfort and understanding. The actual date of this incident is not included in the case study, so the incident could, perhaps, have happened before a Key Person Approach was in place.

The following quote provides an insight into the formation of human relationships:

> Human relationships are motivated by feelings of intense affection, or of disaffection, by emotions that evaluate shared purposes and interests.
>
> (Ruddy in Trevarthen (2004) p. 1)

Consider and discuss this quote in relation to the provocation above and in relation to your own settings.

Prior to the introduction of the Birth to Three Matters Framework (2002) which recommended allocating a Key Person to each child, many settings had started to introduce Key Workers for the babies and young children attending, as mentioned previously. The experiences of children from birth to three years began to improve following the publication of 'Birth to Three Matters' which was developed because it had been identified, by many, that babies' needs were not being met, especially their emotional needs when attending Early Years settings. All Day Care settings and Nurseries registered as caring for children from birth to three years of age received a copy of the document and Early Years Practitioners working in or managing baby rooms were advised to attend Continual Professional Development (CPD) training. Courses and training were provided specifically for this age group by Local Authority Early Years Teams and private trainers. However, it could be questioned as to whether the role of the Key Person was adequately covered in the training because much of the training was related to personal care and education. Using Birth to Three Matters documentation and DVDs the training did address the importance of intimacy, relationships and use of everyday care routines and experiences as important times for learning. As with all training, it was often attended by the well informed but not by those who would really benefit from attendance.

Many Early Years Practitioners felt that they had not received sufficient initial training relating to this age group and often, as identified by many, such as Elfer, Goldschmied, Jackson and more recently Goouch and Powell (2013) in their 'Baby Room Project', they felt undervalued and vulnerable. They were often the youngest members of staff too. Baby room staff experienced the attitude that working in the 'baby room' was/is easy, babies only sleep, feed and need changing. How far from the truth this is? It is one of the hardest age groups to work with, as is discussed later in the chapter under the heading of the role of the Key Person.

Sadly, the stand-alone Birth to Three Matters Framework was discontinued by the Government when parts of the content were integrated into the Early Years Foundation Stage (EYFS) in 2008. However, the original publication remains very useful as a reference point for all practitioners, as is the original EYFS that has supporting documentation such as Development Matters (2012), the related DVD, training materials and helpful references to extra resources and reading matter to deepen practitioners' knowledge and understanding of the care and learning needs of very young children. Integrating the two documents also resulted in children being allocated Key Persons until the end of the Reception Class, an excellent development. Please see the list of extra resources suggested for further reading and available on-line, at the end of this chapter and in the reference list.

As stated above, the Key Person approach was fully introduced as a legal requirement for Early Years Settings in 2008 when the Early Years Foundation Stage Framework was fully introduced following a trial introduction with a group of nurseries. The requirement for each child to be allocated a Key Person became statutory, as recorded in Section 3 'The Welfare requirement' under the heading of 'Organisation.'

Each child must be assigned a key person. In childminding settings, the childminder is the key person.

This included

statutory guidance to which providers must have regard.
    The key person should help the baby or child to become familiar with the provision and to feel confident and safe within it, developing a genuine bond with the child (and the child's parents) and offering a settled, close relationship.
    The key person should meet the needs of each child in their care and respond sensitively to their feelings, ideas and behaviour, talking to parents to make sure that the child is being card for appropriately for each family.
                                                                    (EYFS, DfES 2008 p. 37)

Documentation regarding Key Persons has become more concise, with the following statement being included in Section 1 of the EYFS 2017, The learning and development requirements.

1.10. Each child must be assigned a key person (also a safeguarding and welfare requirement – 3.27, p.22). Providers must inform parents and/or carers of the name of the key person, and explain their role, when a child starts attending a setting. The key person must help ensure that every child's learning and care is tailored to meet their individual needs. The key person must seek to engage and support parents and/or carers in guiding their child's development at home. They should also help families engage with more specialist support if appropriate.

(EYFS 2017 p. 10)

and in Section 3

The Safeguarding and Welfare Requirements

3.27. Each child must be assigned a key person. Their role is to help ensure that every child's care is tailored to meet their individual needs (in accordance with paragraph 1.10), to help the child become familiar with the setting, offer a settled relationship for the child and build a relationship with their parents.

These statements have been included in the EYFS Framework since the 2012 publication.

Implementation and management of the Key Person Approach

The Key Person Approach, as stated above, became mandatory in 2008. As stated at the beginning of this chapter, the importance of a significant adult has been understood since, the work of Bowlby and colleagues in the 1950s and 1960s. It stems from the identified need of every very young child to form close attachments with a significant adult, the Mother, carer or Key Person. The Key Person Approach in an Early Years Setting should result initially in the emotional needs of each baby or young child being met by their Key Person combined with their care and educational needs. The expectations of the Key Person Approach are that the Key Person will form a close attachment bond with each of their key children and with the parents and family. It is through this attachment bond that each baby or young child will be able to settle, to feel accepted, to be reassured, to become familiar with the surroundings and begin to explore, play and learn.

It is well recognised that new concepts and approaches resulting in significant changes to practice can result in some element of resistance from members of staff. It is at these times of changes to practice that managers should not only consider the needs of the children but also the needs of the staff. Strong but sensitive, well informed management of the team is required. Distant support was available, as already mentioned, through training and through texts such as those produced by Manning- Morton and Thorpe (2006) entitled 'Key Times, a Framework for Developing High Quality Provision for Children from Birth to Three.' This publication was closely aligned with and supported the requirements of the framework Birth to Three Matters. It helped to provide support for Key Persons in Early Years settings caring for children from birth to three years. However, it did not provide that immediate support for staff that is often required when experiencing difficult situations within the Early Years setting.

Reflection 1

Consider the following:

How is the Key Person Approach implemented in the different early years settings?

When does the process begin?

What are the constraints that different settings might have?

How are these constraints to be overcome?

Reflect on the approach in your own settings and consider areas for improvement.

The different methods of implementation and management of the approach will be linked to the form of Early Years care and education provided, for example, by maintained nurseries, private and voluntary settings such as full day care, parent run pre-schools and childminders. Each setting will have constraints that affect its approach and many settings have struggled, and still do struggle, with this concept. This struggle can be due to the day-to-day demands of a setting, such as staffing, rapid turnover of staff, shift patterns to cover a ten-hour day, pack away settings, the concerns of staff that they will become too attached to the children, staff illness, holidays and planning the dynamics within a group. Although it must be stated that, once well-established, the Key Person approach leads to a calm environment where there is an involvement, an individual and reciprocal commitment between a member of staff and a family (Elfer et al. 2003). It has also been determined that staff turnover and staff absences are reduced. Key Persons begin to feel valued and part of the team.

This is an approach that develops and changes over time. As stated by Elfer et al. (2003);

It is the process of working and struggling together to:

■ Hear everyone's point of view

■ Help each other develop ideas and possibilities

■ Put proposals into practice and try them out

■ Build on what seems to work and to find another way when something does not.

(Elfer et al. 2003 p. 33)

Case study 1

During a recent conversation with a pre-school manager about managing the Key Person Approach it was acknowledged that because the operating hours were between 09.30 and 14.30 for four days each week during term-time only, they did not experience many the constraints related to full day care when allocating Key Persons. The benefits mentioned were:

■ Continuity for the children and staff

■ All holidays were taken during the school holidays

■ Everyone worked the same hours

■ The children and staff were all in one room, therefore transitions between rooms did not happen.

It meant that the children could remain with the same Key Person throughout their time at the Pre-School. It was also possible, and was requested by staff, that should siblings be attending, the same Key Person would be allocated to those siblings, a practice that was greatly appreciated by children, parents and staff.

Unforeseen events such as staff sickness and occurrences such as being selected for Jury Service still arose, as with any setting. For example, the manager shared the following incident. A Key Person had been called for Jury Service, this commenced only a week after two children, siblings, had started attending the setting. The notification came through to the Key Person after the settling-in visits had commenced. The older sibling, a four-year-old, had appeared to develop a relatively strong, albeit early, relationship with the Key Person who was then away for three weeks. Another member of staff had undertaken the role during the absence and the child was now showing a strong bond to that person. On returning to the setting, the child would not allow the original Key Person to be nearby and would not interact. The child was observed looking at the Key Person with much suspicion and mistrust.

This was a difficult situation for the manager, the Key Person and, most importantly, the child and the parents. The Key Person felt that the child had been let down and the child's trust had been broken. During the Key Person's absence, another member of staff took on the role and ultimately became the child's Key Person. The children's parents were kept informed about the situation and the reasons for the child finding it difficult to settle into the setting.

As you all know, changing a Key Person in a situation like this is not always the best solution for the setting in that the allocation of Key Persons is worked out so that the number of key children for each Key Person is relatively equal. However, the needs of each child must take priority in reflection on the events and discussions within the setting with the setting manager, with the parents and, when appropriate, with the child concerned. There are other times when it is not possible to maintain equal numbers of key children, such as when a new member of staff arrives or when a Key Person is 'off sick.' Most settings include actions within their policies to manage such situations. New members of staff should have an induction period when they may shadow another Key Person prior to taking on that role. Key Persons may partner one another to provide continuity should one or the other be away – sometimes termed a 'buddy system.'

Reflection 2

Consider the case study above:

- How would you have managed the situation?

- Have you had a similar situation and what was the outcome?

- Would you have managed either your own situation or the above scenario differently in the light of experience and your reflections?

Generally, in most Early Years settings, once a place and start date has been allocated to a child, following visits to the setting of choice, it is usual practice for the child to be assigned a Key Person. At this point in time, the Key Person and manager will meet the parent/s/carer/s and child to discuss the child's needs and the parents' requests. The first meetings usually take place in the setting and during these first meetings at the Early Years setting the child will be able to play, or remain with the parent/carer whilst mandatory administration is completed or explained for the parent/carer to complete at home and return at the following visit. Prior to starting at the setting, a home visit may also be arranged and take place. These home visits are ideally set up when two members of staff are available to attend. This should be the Key Person plus another. However, this may not always be possible. It may be the practice in some settings for home visits to take place after the child has started to attend the setting.

It is during the initial visits to the Early Years setting and during the home visits that the Manager and Key Person will observe the reactions of the child and parent/carer to the environment, the other children and the resources and the interactions between the parent/carer and child. These observations should be recorded and used along with information provided by the parent/carer to monitor the child's initial needs, especially his/her emotional needs. the way the child is settling and his/her future care, emotional and developmental needs.

In some Early Years settings, a Key Person is not allocated to new children until the children have attended for a few weeks because the staff observe which member of staff each child appears to be comfortable with. Given the way the Key Person Approach has been discussed up to this point, one may challenge this approach. How is the transition from one setting to another managed; who will help to welcome the child and enable him or her to settle; who will provide the emotional support that is so necessary at this often very difficult time?

When a strong Key Person Approach has been implemented in an Early Years setting the children can be observed to be welcomed each day by their Key Person, parents will be listened to and respected and transitions will be managed calmly, with both children and parents being given time to settle and time with their Key Person. During the day, each child will be supported by their Key Person and spend time one to one and, perhaps, in key groups. The activities provided within the setting will reflect the children's interests and be readily available each day. The Key Persons will remain close by and engaged with their key children to ensure their key children feel safe, secure and able to explore and play. The Key Person is providing, and the child *is experiencing a close relationship that is affectionate and reliable* Elfer et al. (2003 p. 18).

The transition at the end of the day will be managed by the Key Person greeting the parent, providing an exchange of information and each child being reunited with their parent/carer. As with the greeting in the morning or beginning of the child's session, the departure should be calm and not rushed. The child should be given time to adjust to the parent's/carer's presence, to finish their play, their interaction with friends and to say goodbye to their Key Person, all preparation for a transition and the journey home.

The role of the Key Person

Trevarthen believes:

> that the intensely shared pleasure of pride in knowledge and the skill that others applaud, as well as the feeling of shame in failure that threatens loss of relationship and hopeless isolation, are as important to the mental health of every human being as the emotions that seek comfort and care for the body. Indeed, I would suggest that attachment itself, if it is a friendship and not just the very asymmetric relationship between a weak and immature 'patient' and sensitive caregiver, is animated by emotions of shared discovery and the creation of inventive art.
>
> (Trevarthen 2004 p. 9)

This will be revisited later in the chapter but try to keep it in mind as you continue to read and consider your role as a Key Person because the quote relates closely to the role.

The EFYS and other sources, like Trevarthen above, give an outline of the role of the Key Person but do not really address how it will be made to work in practice, especially when one considers the different Early Years settings that young children may attend.

Reflection 3

When does the role of the Key Person begin in your setting?
   How are key children allocated?
   Consider the reasons why children are allocated to certain members of staff.

The role of the Key Person will now be explored in more detail with references being made to the quote at the beginning of this section.

The Key Person is there to:

- Welcome key children and their parents/carers

- Create a warm welcoming environment where each child's interests are provided for and reflected in the resources that are readily available and sit at the children's level

- Respond readily to the needs of each key child, maintain eye contact, mimic sounds of younger babies, repeat phrases and statements from older children to show you have heard and understood

- Listen to the children and their parents/carers

- Build strong, close (Manning-Morton, Thorpe 2006), reciprocal, trusting, knowledgeable relationships with the key children and their families

- Understand the different cultural approaches to parenting and the parents'/carers' expectations of the Early Years Setting

- Complete, record and analyse regular observations of their key children

- Include the observations in the child's personal documentation

- Share information with other professionals who may be involved in the care and education of the child

- Provide information to parents/carers regarding extra support that maybe required by the family

- Share with the child their successes and progression

- Share with and support the child when he/she is upset because they have experienced a sense of failure in their voyage of discovery, their play

- Work closely with parents to resolve situations when a child may require extra support

- Plan and provide for the care routines for their key children, having discussed these with the parents/carers. Does the child have a comforter, like to be cuddled to sleep, like food chopped, mashed or pureed etc., etc. Maintain the home routine for eating and sleeping whilst at the Early Years Setting

- Plan and provide play experiences based on the knowledge gained from parents and observations of their key children's individual interests and learning needs.

The activities listed above can be identified and simplified under the key aspects of a Key Person relationship in the 'Key Times Framework' as the Key Person should:

- *Be available*

- *Be tuned-in*

- *Be responsive*

- *Be consistent.*

(Manning-Morton and Thorpe 2006 pp. 86–87)

Reflection 4

Can you relate your role as a Key Person to the need for a secure base?

Do you as a Key Person provide the secure base that is so necessary to enable very young children to settle and to develop, and do you also, as identified by Holmes (2001) provide the 'empathy and responsiveness' that is required to ensure that children's emotional needs are observed, recognised and met?

(Johnson 2016 p. 235)

Consider these two questions and refer to Chapter 2 on attachment theory where the need for a secure base is addressed in more detail. It is so important for the Key Person to be able to provide empathy and responsiveness to meet the emotional needs of their key children, to be able to share the moments of achievement – that shared pleasure – as well as moments when the key child is experiencing a sense of failure, as identified by Trevarthen (2004, p. 9) in the quote above under the heading 'The Role of the Key Person. He speaks of attachment as being *animated by emotions of shared discovery and the creation of inventive art.* Is this occurring when you are *making friends with* your key children?

Now relate the thoughts of Trevarthen to the provision that you might create within your Early Years setting to ensure the interests and learning needs of your key children are being met. Are you aware of the *'emotions of shared discovery and the creation of inventive art'?* How will you plan to ensure there is reciprocity and enjoyment?

Reflection 5

How do you observe your key children?

How do you plan and use the information gained from the observations?

Do you see the experiences of the children and yourself as a journey together?

How do you meet the inherent need of very young children to explore and discover within each environment they experience?

How do you use the information gained from parents/carers?

Do you value free flow play?

Do you enjoy and appreciate the importance of outdoor play?

How do you ensure children have access to these experiences?

Within the role of the Key Person, observations and planning play have been mentioned. Holistic observations and free flow play, particularly outdoor play, are briefly discussed here in order that you can appreciate the values of both and link them into your role, reflect on your practice and possibly implement changes in your Early Years settings. The content of the observations you have recorded should ensure that you respond to the interests and learning needs of your key children. Areas of learning have not been specified here because each child should be observed, analysed and assessed holistically. As Reid (1999) emphasizes, you should observe what is seen and not what you think you should see. The Tavistock Model of infant observation also teaches that the observer should not take notes but record what has been seen as soon after the observation as possible.

Consider the following interpretation of the six gifts developed by Frederick Froebel, that link to the mathematically designed Block Play we have today.

Froebel saw these gifts not as a present given, but a tool which would help children to indicate their gifts so that the adult would know which areas of a child's interest and understanding to encourage.

(in Liebschner 1992 p. 71)

In other words, observing the way the children play with the 'gifts' provides the observer with important information about the child; the children are demonstrating their interests and abilities. Have you been provided with gifts? The gifts provided during observations enable the Key Person to respond to a child's actual needs not what they think the child needs (Gerhardt 2004). It is only by observing children holistically that we can truly learn about all areas of their development. If we just concentrate on each area of development in turn we will miss vital areas of development and particularly the emotional needs of the children. In psychoanalytical terms, the Key Person should develop the skill of containment by 'suspending our own needs and wishes in favour of those of another' (Reid 1999 p. 3), thus providing love and care for your key children whilst in your settings. The role of the Key Person is, as already mentioned throughout this chapter, very challenging. At this point you may wish to refer to Chapter 2 on attachment theory and the effects of separation. Once a child has settled into a setting he/she should be able to explore and play.

Child care and educational pioneers such as Rousseau, Froebel and Isaacs believed in children having freedom to play, especially experiencing outdoor play where the activities are mostly open ended. Children should be able to explore, climb, dig, create dens, puddle jump, and discover everything about the world around them. Outdoor play provides children with the opportunities to progress their all-round development through physical activity, learning about and connecting with nature, science, mathematics and expanding their language and literacy skills. Outdoor play enables them to be creative and use their imaginative skills to further develop their play and make sense of the world around them. Blocks can be used indoors and outdoors; they result in play that is completely open-ended. However, for the play with blocks to be completely fulfilling it is imperative that the blocks are mathematically designed. Froebel's gifts 3–6 consisted of small blocks that developed in their complexity but were divided into multiples of eight. The blocks can be linked closely to nature because many flowers resemble 'geometric forms' Read (1992) and have eight petals; symmetrical patterns can be created in two-dimensional and three-dimensional designs or as marquetry, towers, roads, houses and cars; trains can be built and the blocks can represent anything a child wishes them to represent. For further information and a description of the gifts please see Tovey, *Bringing the Froebel Approach to your Early Years Practice* (2013 pp. 45–49).

> ### Reflection 6
>
> Having read the examples of open-ended play above, reflect on the activities provided in your settings:
>
> Are they open-ended and exciting?
>
> Would you enjoy playing with them?
>
> What resources would you provide that are open-ended?
>
> What resources would you remove from your setting and why?

Block play and outdoor play have been chosen as examples of open-ended play because there is increasing evidence about the value of open-ended play, Tovey (2008), Solly (2015), and the impact on the learning abilities of children who are not exposed to the outdoors but spend their time *'glued'* to computer screens, tablets and mobile phones. The children become rather like zombies, unable to function and bored when they do not have a moving screen in front of them; they have become addicted to the screen. A common scenario in conversation with parents of very young children who have been allowed to play with tablets is that the tablets have been taken away, because of the children's unwanted behaviours, temper tantrums and inability to play imaginatively with their toys and with their siblings. Almost as soon as the tablets are banned or their use restricted the children have started to play with their toys, enjoy being outside and being creative.

Sitting most of the time and not experiencing physical activity also leads to other health problems, such as childhood obesity, which in time can lead to heart disease and type 2 diabetes. Type 2 diabetes has been identified in younger children and is linked to obesity (Solly 2015 and Rose et al. 2016). Furthermore, very serious issues were identified by Byron (2008) who wrote a report on the dangers for children of using electronic devices that link directly to the internet, exposing them to inappropriate films, bullying on-line by their peers and the potential grooming by paedophiles.

It is not being suggested that Early Years settings allow children to sit for long periods of time at computers or that the computers are not protected; they are. It is not being suggested either, that children should not be able to use technology given that we live in a technological age, although, in many settings, such as Steiner Nurseries, they are not used at all (House 2011) or are discouraged, as are plastic toys. The reason computers and technology have been mentioned is because they are one of the issues within early years today and discussion of them reinforces the importance of the Key Person's multifaceted role. This is a possible topic of conversation that may arise when speaking to parents/carers. It is also discussed in Chapter 5. You may be able to advise on the use of safe programmes or websites for children. You may also be able to encourage parents to increase the physical activities their child is involved in, for example walking rather than driving to your setting, or suggest clubs such as football, tennis clubs, music and movement, gymnastics or dancing classes that the children can join as they reach the appropriate age. Your expertise and previous experience is invaluable to parents and other members of staff within the setting. It should also help to improve provision for the children if they are not able to access the outdoors in the Early Years setting or at home.

The EYFS (2017) requires that, where possible, children should experience open access to the outdoors so that their play flows from inside to outdoors. Having specific times for outdoor play is discouraged; children should have the choice to play inside or outside at any time. If there is no outdoor area, then outdoor activities should be arranged for the children each day.

> 3.58. Providers must provide access to an outdoor play area or, if that is not possible, ensure that outdoor activities are planned and taken on a daily basis (unless circumstances make this inappropriate, for example unsafe weather conditions). Providers must follow their legal responsibilities under the Equality Act 2010 (for example, the provisions on reasonable adjustments).
>
> (EYFS 2017 3.58 p. 30)

Children who have access to the outdoors and engage with nature have been found to have more advanced development. Their physical skills are enhanced, their general health is better in that they are ill less often, and their cognitive skills are improved, as discussed by Solly (2015). Access to outdoors play has also been shown to enhance children's emotional development, making them more sensitive towards their peers (Moore 1986, in Solly 2015); these children are much calmer. Froebel (1837, in Liebschner (1992), Bruce et al (2012) and Tovey (2013)

When children are allowed to develop their own free flow play, where one minute they may be playing in the home corner and the next moment they may have taken stones or small blocks that they use as fruits or vegetables, or even jewels, and transport them around in handbags, their general sense of emotional well-being is enhanced. This is certainly evident during their enjoyment of exploration and discovery, the play that is collaborative and open-ended, along with the open - ended resources provided indoors and by the outdoors. They are involved in their play. The presence of a Key Person who is observing, providing guidance when it is required and not leading the play but enjoying the children's experiences at the same time, is invaluable. Froebel (1837 in Liebschner (1992), Bruce et al. (2012) and Tovey (2013) identify this response of the adult as providing *freedom with guidance*, which is explored in more detail in Chapter 5. Both the key child and children and you your-self can discover and be creative together, thus forming strong bonds with each other. In direct opposition to this is the occasion when an Early Years Practitioner interrupts play, for example where children are prevented from transporting 'jewels' because they, the 'jewels', must be kept in the designated area of the nursery. This could be a lost opportunity; instead, the children could be asked, by a different Practitioner to return them to the area they had been taken from at the end of their game.

Before moving on to consider the impact of being a Key Person on you your-self and the supervision and support that you may require, here are two different activities for you to consider. Provocation 2a, a group of three one–year-old babies playing with large cardboard boxes and Provocation 2b, a group of children com-pleting a set piece of artwork – creating their own picture. These examples are taken from practical experience

---

Provocation 2a

A group of babies was playing with cardboard boxes following the delivery of Nursery equipment. The contents had been removed and the babies could not be seen!! They were sitting in the boxes that had been turned onto their sides. Two babies had crawled right to the back of one of the boxes whilst the other sat half way inside another box. A short game of peek-a-boo followed with the three babies who roared with laughter each time they popped their heads or whole bodies out of the boxes. They played in this way crawling in and out, looking, as described by Trevarthen (2004), chuffed with their success of crawling in and out, for the majority of the day and in fact for many of the following days. What a pleasure to observe. Their success and enjoyment were being acknowledged by their Key Persons.

Provocation 2b

It is the beginning of the new academic year when many new children arrive in settings. The children who are three years old are asked to create a picture of themselves. They are given a paper plate, different coloured pens and pencils and different coloured wools. The children create their eyes, either blue, green or brown by using pre-cut circles of tissue paper. Their noses are painted with white paint and their mouths are red and then they glue the appropriate coloured wool to represent their hair. Activity over, the results are displayed on the appropriate display board.

Compare and contrast these two activities, perhaps share them with your col-leagues and discuss the merits of each. Consider the learning that was taking place and the schemas that may have been observed, particularly in Provocation 2a. Also, research on-line for a poem called 'the Little Boy'

http://myjc.jc.edu/users//holley/LittleBoy.htm (accessed 12 December 2017)

The poem is very powerful, and it is very sad. Discuss this poem and provocation 2b. What is happening to the children and what is the impact of such adult led activities? How will you as a Key Person avoid this situation and the resultant loss of the ability of the child to use his or her own imagination.

The reason for including activities such as block play, open-ended play and outdoor play here within the role of the Key Person is because of issues linked to the modern culture of being 'risk averse' and the health and wellbeing of our children. Many articles appear in the National Press as well as Early Years journals discussing these points. The topic is discussed above and is discussed and analysed further in Chapter 5.

Difficulties that may occur for Key Persons

Many of the difficulties that Key Persons may experience have been included in the provocations, case study and reflections within this chapter to enable you to think about the important role a Key Person has in the lives of the children and families with whom they work. You will have read that it is not an easy role and how very demanding and stressful it can be. Many Practitioners and Key Persons feel undervalued, as identified by Elfer et al. (2003) and Goouch and Powell (2013). This has been found to be especially so in the baby room, where the youngest members of staff often work because managers perceive the work to be easy. A baby's continuous crying is very emotive to most adults and being able to console a very small baby can, at times, prove to be extremely hard despite years of experience and a calm manner. You may not be able to respond to a particular child's needs however hard you try. One of your key children may always go to another member of your team. A parent may have made a complaint, shown hostility and demanded that a new Key Person is appointed. This is discussed further in Chapter 4, 'Working with Parents', many of whom have reservations about the relationship a Key Person may develop with their child or children.

Reflection 7

Consider the following points and reflect on the meaning of professional love (Page 201 1a)

■ Will the relationship, for you, be too close and will it be too close for the Mother?

■ When you have developed a strong bond with each of your key children, how will you feel when they move to a new room in your setting, move on to school or move away from the area?

■ How will this separation affect you?

■ How do you maintain the professionalism that is so important when working with people, especially children?

These questions all raise the issue about who you turn to for help and guidance when you are, perhaps, finding it hard to work with your key children. Do you work in a well organised setting where regular supervision and support is factored in by management? Do you work in a setting where you, returning to the quote by Elfer et al.:

■ Hear everyone's point of view

■ Help each other develop ideas and possibilities

■ Put proposals into practice and try them out

■ Build on what seems to work and find another way when something does not.

(Elfer et al 2003 p. 33)

Supervision and support for Key Persons

The importance of your Key Person role has been expressed throughout this chapter. Sometimes this must have felt daunting but at the same time you might be thinking, 'well we do have a good Key Person Approach in our setting.' The question of supervision and support for you by your line manager or a designated, experienced Key Person will now be addressed. The enormity of your role and the responsibility you have as a Key Person and the related stress experienced in this role must not be overlooked. It has been identified earlier in this chapter and by other researchers that Early Years Practitioners often feel very alone and undervalued in their settings and especially so as a Key Person. Conversely, if the approach is well implemented and the setting is calm, you will feel valued and you will feel much closer to your key children and their families. You will have a sense of achievement and feel part of the team.

In using the term 'supervision', your immediate thought is possibly, 'oh, I am going to be observed to ensure I am fulfilling my role.' This is not the purpose of supervision, if it is implemented in the correct way. It is in place to provide you with support, for you to be able to discuss your key children and for you to raise any concerns you may have about their progress and their health and emotional well-being. You may wish to discuss information that has been shared with you by other relations or carers, that is of concern to you and which you may have discussed before without reaching any conclusions about your concerns or whether there were real causes for concern. To meet regularly to discuss such issues, knowing that confidentiality will be maintained, is very supportive. It provides the opportunity to consider the needs of your key children in a calm, uninterrupted manner. It is your time to be listened to and heard, which will enable you to respond to the individual needs of each baby and very young child.

This is also a time to discuss you own feelings of stress, happiness, sadness and how you will cope with them and of how you will cope with forming close relationships with the children and their families. In well led supervision, the meetings will take place regularly, perhaps every two weeks or once each month. These meetings will provide time for discussion and for reflection in order to move forward from the situation.

Elfer et al. see a supervision system as 'essential for each Early Years Setting . . . to retain professional boundaries . . . and to provide staff with trained support in recognition of their complex and sophisticated work with children and families'(Elfer et al. 2003 p. 59).

Elfer also proposed that the:

> Quality of fit between the needs of the babies and their families and the particular circumstances and resources of each staff member is a very complex and intricate interaction.
>
> (Elfer 2004, paper presented at Pen Green)

This complex interaction, if understood and supported by the management, through supervision, should result in staff being able to respond to the emotional needs of the children in their Key Groups more easily, because their own needs have been responded to.

Reflection 8

- Do you yourselves feel supported in your role as a Key Person?

- Are there times when you would like more support?

- If you receive support, how is this given?

- How would you be able to support the staff in your setting to develop their ability to respond to the emotional and developmental needs of their key children?

Conclusion

Throughout this chapter the focus has been the importance of your role as a Key Person who is required to form a strong reciprocal relationship with each of your key children and their families. This is a relationship that has a lasting impact on the future development of each child, the rapid development of the brain and the formation of neural connections through secure attachments and experiences that are formed in the first three years of life and linked to their emotional need to feel safe and secure. As Dowling (2010) states, *'Babies' brains thrive on companionship'* (p. 81) and supported by Trevarthen (1998) who speaks about children 'needing company which is interested and curious and affectionate . . .' (in Dowling 2010, p. 81). The provision of play experiences that promote physical development, especially during outdoor play, which in turn promotes the development of communication and language, personal, social and emotional development, literacy, mathematics, understanding the world, expressive arts and design – the seven areas of learning in EYFS 2017 have been covered. Remember, Goddard Blythe gave the derivative of emotion as *emovere*, Latin meaning 'to move.' This relates to planning that you will be involved in but also to the current issues in Early Years that are regularly in the news. Most of these issues are related to the health and wellbeing of our society due to our more sedentary lifestyle and the use of technology.

Whilst the main focus has been on the emotional needs of the children and how the Key Person Approach may be implemented, positive and negative issues have been considered from the position of the Key Person. Early Years settings where the Key Person Approach is in place and supervision has been provided for staff have been highlighted as having quality provision Elfer (2003). This is because staff who are closely supported in their role will be assisted and enabled to form vital responsive relationships with their key children.

The opportunity to extend your knowledge and understanding of your professional role as a Key Person can be researched further through the following suggested reading.

Further reading

Elfer, P (2012) Emotion in nursery work: Work Discussion as a model of critical professional reflection in *Early Years, an International Journal of Research and Development*, Volume 32, Number 2, July 2012, Oxon: Routledge.

This paper was prepared following research into the impact of responding to the emotional needs of the children on the Early Years workforce, especially Key Persons. Elfer refers to their work as *'emotional labour'* when trying to *'evoke or suppress emotions'* in many of the daily routines while working in partnership with parents. Elfer poses many issues for debate that may help you to reflect on your practice in many of the diverse situations that may arise in your settings.

Reid, S Ed. (1997) *Developments in Infant Observation, The Tavistock Model* London: Routledge.

This book is written for psychotherapists. However, there are points that will help you as Key Persons. It highlights the importance of in-depth observations that record the actions and interactions of infants and their Mothers/carers. The observers are encouraged to record exactly what they observe and not what they think they should be observing, a point that has been made within this Chapter. Far more is learned about babies and young children when this approach is taken, especially when the content of observations is interpreted, discussed, analysed and then used to provide for the individual child's care and learning needs. Consider the way you observe your key children in relation to the technique explained above and within this chapter.

Page, J (2011b) Do mothers want professional carers to love their babies? In *Journal of Early Childhood Research 9 (3)* London: Sage.

This paper, along with other writings by Page, focuses mainly on the wishes of Mothers when leaving their babies and children with carers such as a nanny, childminder or in group settings. It highlights some of the dilemmas that have been discussed in this chapter and will also provide insight into concerns about the relationships their children may have with Key Persons. It will provide information about providing professional love and maintaining a professional stance when working with parents, as discussed in Chapter 4.

Quan-McGimpsey, S; Kuczynski, L; Brophy, K (2011) Early education teachers' conceptualizations and strategies for managing closeness in child care: The personal domain in *Journal of Early Childhood Research 9: 232* originally published online 21 April 2011 ECR: Sage, accessed on line 13 December 17.

This paper provides a contrast to the approach by Page regarding professional love. The research focuses on the intimate relationships that can form between a teacher and a child. It also links to the paper by Elfer on emotional labour.

Roberts, R (2010) *Self-Esteem and Early Learning – Key People from Birth to School*, London: Sage.

This book takes into consideration all of the Key People in a baby's and young child's life. It includes but does not focus purely on the role of the Key Person. Scenarios are included about each of the Key People which will help you to reflect on your own role and the fact that collaboration between Key People is essential. It also provides links to the other chapters in this book. As well as reflection, it encourages analysis and critique.

References

Bligh, C; Chambers, S; Davison, C; Lloyd, I; Musgrave, J; O'Sullivan, J and Waltham, S (2013) *Well-being in the Early Years* Northwich: Critical Publishing

Bruce, T; Baker, M; Brown, S; Bruce, T; McNair, L; McCormick, C; Ouvry, M; Read, J; Spratt, J; Tovey, T and Whinnett, J (2012) *Early Childhood Practice – Froebel Today*, London; Sage

Davison, C (2013) The Parents' and Extended Family Perspective in Bligh, C et al (2013) *Well-being in the early Years* Northwich: Critical Publishing

DCSF (2008) *The Byron Review – Children and New Technology*, Nottingham DCSF Publications

DfE (2012) *The Statutory Framework for the Early Years Foundation Stage*, Runcorn: DfE accessed on line March 2014

DfE (2014) *The Statutory Framework for the Early Years Foundation Stage*, Runcorn: DfE accessed on line March 2014

DfE (2017) *The Statutory Framework for the Early Years Foundation Stage*, Runcorn: DfE accessed on line March 2017

DfES (2002) *Birth to Three Matters*, London: DfES Publications

DfES (2008) *The Early Years Foundation Stage*, London: DfES Publications

Dowling, M (2010) 3rd Ed *Young Children's Personal, Social and Emotional Development*, London: Paul Chapman

Elfer, P (2004) The importance to infants of a keyperson who is well supervised and supported, Research paper presented at Pen Green 3 July 2004.

Elfer, P (2012) Emotion in nursery work: Work Discussion as a model of critical professional reflection in *Early Years, an International Journal of Research and Development*, Volume 32, Number 2, July 2012, Oxon: Routledge

Elfer, P; Goldschmied, E; Selleck, D (2003) *Key Persons in the Nursery*, London: David Fulton

Gerhardt, S (2004) *Why Love Matters*, East Sussex: Brunner-Routledge

Goldschmied, E; Jackson, S (2004) *People Under Three*, 2nd Ed London: Routledge

Goouch, K; Powell, S (2013) *The Baby Room*, Berkshire: Oxford University Press

Hay, S (1997) *Essential Nursery Management*, London: Bailliere and Tindall

Holmes, J (2001) *The Search for the Secure Base*, East Sussex; Brunner-Routledge

House, R (ed.) (2011) *Too Much, Too Soon?* Gloucestershire: Hawthorn Press

Johnson, T (2016) Holistic Development: The Social and Emotional Needs of Children, in *The Early Years Handbook for Students and Practitioners*, ed. Trodd, L; Oxon: Routledge

Liebschner, J (1992/2001) *A Child's Work, Freedom and Guidance in Froebel's Educational Theory and Practice* Cambridge: Lutterworth Press

Manning-Morton, J and Thorp, M (2006) *Key Times A Framework for Developing High Quality Provision for Children from Birth to Three*, Maidenhead: Open University

Page, J (2011a) Do mothers want professional carers to love their babies? In *Journal of Early Childhood Research 9 (3)* pp. 310–323 London: Sage

Page, J (2011b) *Professional Love in Early Years Settings: A Report of the Summary of Findings* https://www.bing.com/search?q=Jools+Page+Professional+Love+2011&src=IE SearchBox&FORM=IESR4S&pc=EUPP_UE02 accessed 27 February 2018

Quan-McGimpsey, S; Kuczynski, L; Brophy, K (2011) Early education teachers' conceptualizations and strategies for managing closeness in child care: The personal domain in *Journal of Early Childhood Research 9: 232* originally published online 21 April 2011 ECR: Sage, accessed on line 13.12.17

Read, J (1992) A short History of Children's Building Blocks in *Exploring Learning Young Children and Blockplay*, London: Paul Chapman Publishing ed. Gura, P

Reber, A S (1995) *The Penguin Dictionary of Psychology*. London: Penguin

Reid, S (1997) *Developments in Infant Observations, The Tavistock Model*. London: Routledge

Roberts, R (2010) *Self-Esteem and Early Learning – Key People from Birth to School*, London: Sage

Rose, J, Gilbert, L, Richards, V (2016) *Health and Wellbeing in Early Childhood*. London: Sage

Solly, K (2015) *Risk, Challenge and Adventure in the Early Years*, Oxon: Routledge

Tovey, H (2008) *Playing Outdoors Spaces and Places Risk and Challenge* Maidenhead: OU Press

Tovey, H (2013) *Bringing the Froebel Approach to your Early Years Practice*, Oxon: Routledge

Trevarthen, C (2002) Learning in Companionship in *Education in the North: The Journal of Scottish Education*, New Series, Number 10, 2002, pp.16–25

Trevarthen, C (2004, July) *Making Friends with Infants* Paper presented at Penn Green Conference: Northampton.

Websites

http://myjc.jc.edu/users//holley/LittleBoy.htm accessed on-line 19.09.17

www.aimh.org.uk

www.education.gov.uk/publications

www.legislation.gov.uk/

www.sciencemediacentre.org/expert-reaction-to-the-biological-effects-of-day-care-as-published-in-the-biologist-a-journal-of-the-society-of-biology-2-

www.uni.edu/universitas/archive/fall06/pdf/art_praglin.pdf

www.webarchives.gov.uk

4 Working with parents

Key themes in this chapter

After reading this chapter you should be able to:

■ Discuss the importance of forming close partnerships with the parents of your key children

■ Analyse and critique the challenges you may experience

■ Reflect upon your listening and hearing skills when working with parents and colleagues

■ Use your reflections to implement possible new approaches to forming collaborative partnerships with parents

■ Ensure that all parents are respected and valued

■ Analyse the effects of valuing parents on the emotional needs of the babies and young children who attend your settings

■ Maintain a professional approach to all aspects of your work with your key children and their parents

■ Fully relate your role as a Key Person to forming strong, collaborative partnership with parents.

Introduction

Forming strong, collaborative partnerships and easily accessible, strong lines of communication with parents is one of the most important roles of the Key Person.

It could, perhaps, be said that it is one of the most rewarding aspects of your work with children. Discussion and analysis of the bonds of attachment with your key children are covered in detail in Chapters 2 and 3 but are briefly revisited in this chapter, along with the strong partnerships that are formed when more than one child in a family attends the setting. This special relationship is a privilege. However, the challenges that occur within the formation of relationships and partnerships are addressed before looking at the process of developing a partnership.

Throughout the chapter the following themes relating to forming partnerships with parents are explored in more detail. They include the importance of listening to and hearing parents and carers, especially concerning information that is directly related to the needs of the child, which could change almost daily – listening to and hearing parents' and carers' requests and their completely new information about their baby or young child, such as changes to the named person collecting them at the end of a session, changes to routine or health needs or any concerns they may have. Consideration is given to ensuring that the daily routines of babies, very young children and children with complex needs, are followed and prioritised. The importance of ensuring that parents and carers and their children are valued and acknowledging the knowledge that each parent/carer has about their child and being able to recognise each parent/carer as their child's first educator, Whalley (2001), McDowell Clark (2017) are discussed in detail. Every area within a partnership that will impact on the emotional and developmental needs of babies and young children if the partnership with their parents of carers is not established and maintained is included.

The opportunity for reflection and discussion about the different experiences Early Years' Practitioners may have encountered when working with parents/carers and their children is included. You, as Early Years Practitioners and Key Persons are encouraged to reflect on, to critique and analyse your own practice and your own feelings through the various provocations and case studies that are included. This should help you to ensure that parental partnerships in your settings are strengthened through your approach and that your responses to the parents'/carers' individual needs are all strongly connected to the individual needs of their child/children.

Challenges that may present within partnership with parents

In the way that every baby and young child is unique and therefore has many different needs, with the focus here being primarily in relation to their emotional needs, so too are their parents unique. The way that parents respond to Key Persons/teachers in Early Years settings will be very much linked to their own experiences and relationships during their early years at home, at school, at work and in fact throughout their lives. This has been well researched by psychotherapists and psychologists such as Bowlby (1969), Fonagy (2003) and Nelson-Coffey et al. (2017) in relation to attachment and parenting. Whalley et al (2001), when researching and developing the Pen Green Centre, identified through the Parents Involved in their Children's Learning (PICL) study group, that not every parent or family whose child/children were attending the centre would wish to be involved in their children's learning. The wishes of those who did not want to participate were respected. Good communication between those parents and the setting was maintained and ultimately the Key Persons and researchers 'strong belief was affirmed', that:

> parents are committed to, interested in and excited by their children's learning
> (Whalley 2001 p. 56)

even when they did not wish to, and did not, attend the PICL group.

This positive affirmation should be retained by you as Key Persons because most parents want 'what is best for their child/children' Dowling (2010, p. 192) and there are many reasons why parents may not wish, or be able, to participate fully in the day to day life of a setting and their children's learning.

Among the factors identified by Whalley and the Pen Green Team that were seen to possibly impact on parents' participation and that you might now consider were:

- Marital status

- Parents' employment

- Language barriers

- Family pressures

- Whether the child has one or two years in the nursery

- Whether the parent had a previous child in the nursery

- Parents' apparent hostility to any intervention

- Parents' own education experiences

- The family worker's (nursery nurse's) personality

- Changes in family life (e.g., sickness/pregnancy, etc.)

- Whether the child has special needs or there are other children in the home with special needs

(Whalley 2001 p. 53)

These factors, although related to specific research, are factors that you may often encounter when working with parents. They are referred to and expanded upon throughout this chapter. Alongside these factors it is also important to take into consideration different forms of parenting experienced by each child in your setting. Every household has different values and a different culture compared to that of their neighbour. This theme is explored in more detail in Chapter 5 – The effects of different cultures experienced by very young children. However, this should not impact on Key Persons forming a lasting relationship with parents by finding out more about them, the child and their home. Georgeson and Payler (2013) discuss that fact that the 'informal chats', at the beginning and end of the day, 'were often times when parents shared valuable information' (p. 268). Ward (2016, p. 319) speaks about partnership working 'being built on trust.'

When meeting parents, carers and their children for the first time, during their initial visit to a nursery, day care setting, pre-school or childminder, you, as an Early Years Practitioner, will be very aware that the parent/s/carer/s and their child/children could be feeling very anxious. Conversely, they could feel very excited about their visit and the prospect of moving on into the next phase of their child's life. However, this is possibly the first time they are considering leaving their baby or very young child with someone other than a family member. It may even be the first time they have ever left their baby or very young child. It is also the time when you, as the prospective Key Person, will be very sensitive to the parents' needs, to their body language, facial language and their spoken words. Although, during an initial visit, you will not be directly 'involving the parents in their child's learning', it is your goal to ensure that they, the parent/carer, feel welcomed and acknowledged, and, that they feel their child/children are welcomed and will be appropriately responded to, safe and secure in the setting. Parents and carers do not always bring their baby or young child to the initial visit. However, when they do, you will also be observing the child's reaction to the environment, to you as their prospective Key Person and to the toys/play experiences that are available. You are beginning to learn about the baby/young child and his/her parents/carers and to build the foundations for a strong relationship with the child and a strong partnership with the parents.

Therefore, before exploring the ways that you will create a partnership with new parents, it is pertinent that you should now reflect on and analyse your own feelings when, in the past, you have experienced new, unfamiliar situations. To reflect and acknowledge your own feelings will help you to understand how others might be feeling and enable you to work more easily with others.

Reflection 1

■ Consider your feelings when entering a strange situation for the first time.

■ How did you feel?

■ What emotions did you experience?

■ Did this experience affect you alone or was another person involved?

■ What was the impact on that other person?

■ What strategies did you use to manage the situation?

■ Now consider how a parent or carer might be feeling during their first visit to your setting.

■ How will you work with parents and carers to help them to feel less anxious?

■ Would you consider changing the format for first visits to your setting and if so, what changes would you make?

What advice do you think you might provide for a parent/carer who is visiting your setting for the first time when, during the visit, you perhaps become aware that this is the one and only setting they have chosen to visit and that they are not completely comfortable about the experience? Consider the following brief provocation.

Reflection 2

Experience provides you with expertise in this type of situation. As you are showing them around the parent/carer might say to you,

'well I have heard from my friends that it is really good here.' 'You have had a good or even outstanding Ofsted Inspection, therefore, it must be right for my baby/child to attend here.'

However, you are picking up vibes that although this is being said, it is not how they are feeling.

(continued)

(continued)

- How might you gently question them about their feelings?

- How would you encourage them to go and visit other settings?

- How important do you think it is to visit more than one setting and why?

- What could be the constraints that perhaps prevent another setting from being considered by the parent/carer?

- How would you reassure the parent/carer about their reservations and reasons for feeling unsure?

Most Practitioners would advise parents to visit other Early Years settings and types of care because your setting might not be the right one for them. Perhaps, home care such as a childminder, employing a nanny for themselves or sharing a nanny with another family, could be explored. You might suggest that they contact the Local Authority Early Years Department for lists of names of other Early Years settings and childminders in the area and provide them with the website for the Local Authority, email address or telephone number. Although you support your setting and it is rated as good or outstanding, you must be honest; it might not be the right setting for this family and their baby or very young child. It might just not feel right to them; they may be experiencing a 'gut instinct' that there is some aspect they are not happy with. Very importantly, if a parent or carer is feeling unsure about a setting their baby or young child will feel that uncertainty and consequently may feel emotionally insecure. Although you have been asked to explore the reasons for parents' or carers' reservations, they might not even be able to articulate their feelings. The outcome you are hoping for is that the parents or carers choose the setting that is right for them and, most importantly, their child.

Professionally this is the right advice to give, you are beginning to build a relationship of trust by being open and truthful. However, you may be experiencing a conflict of interest when placed in this position because, as you are all very familiar with, there is pressure for you to maintain the occupancy levels of your setting. This is a situation that is being exacerbated in some settings such as pre-schools and maintained nurseries because of the impact of paying the minimum wage to all staff, the legal requirement to offer pensions to staff and the 30 hours free provision each week for children aged three to four years. Many pre-schools have closed following the implementation of the 15 free hours for children aged from three to four years and the new Early Years National Funding Formula which is linked to the increase to 30 hours free provision. There have been many articles in the national press and *Nursery World* about maintained nurseries and pre-schools being under threat because of the Early Years National Funding Formula (*Nursery World* 11 August 2016)

Although the Government has agreed to provide extra funding for maintained nurseries until the end of its current term (House of Commons Library 2017). The threat to maintained nurseries arises because, currently, local authorities provide the funding to these nurseries and have the autonomy to fund at a higher rate than the funding they will receive once the National Funding Formula is implemented. A point to consider is that many maintained nurseries are in areas of deprivation and disadvantage. They provide an invaluable service to their local communities and have been found to raise the attainment of the children who attend. McDowall Clark (2017 p. 74) quotes Ofsted (2014) who reported this as, 'bucking the trend', which has been achieved because the settings have had 'high expectations for all children.'

Analysis in 2014, recorded in *The State of the Nation*, by the Social Mobility and Child Poverty Commission found that:

Parenting has a bigger influence on a child's life chances in the early years than education, wealth or class

but

Four out of ten children experience poor parenting.

(State of the Nation 2014)

However, the State of the Nation report presented in 2015(HMSO 2014) stated that:

as many as one in six children still spend large parts of their lives living in households which are persistently poor.

This may appear to be a digression from the subject of the emotional needs of babies and very young children and their parents/carers. However, the purpose of this slight digression is to highlight the related challenges, dilemmas and pressures from government initiatives and new research that influences parents' and carers' perception of children's care and educational needs, all of which you may encounter. Consideration should also be given to the importance of employing well qualified, professional members of staff, as identified and recommended in the Nutbrown Review (2012). Nutbrown identified the impact of employing a well-qualified, Early Years graduate in each setting because the standards of childcare and education experienced by the children were found to be of higher quality than those settings who did not have graduate members of staff. Again there are cost implications.

The recommendation to employ a graduate in each setting could be discussed and analysed in relation to each specific setting because staff qualified to level 3 in Childcare and Education, with many years of experience, who have had their own families, are able to provide an 'Outstanding' level of provision (taken from knowledge of a recent Ofsted report 2017 for a pre-school which was rated 'Outstanding' and where the majority of the staff are qualified to level 3). Having given that last example and having vast practical experience lecturing in Further Education and Higher Education it must be said that most graduates do bring a very much deeper level and breadth of understanding of the all-round development of very young children and the needs of parents to the settings in which they work. They can be more innovative, have better, informed, management skills and knowledge, including developing strong, respectful partnerships with parents and other professionals. They have a breadth of knowledge of the different childcare and educational approaches, the related theorists such as Bowlby, Bruner, Piaget, Vygotsky and the Early Years Pioneers such as Froebel, Montessori and Steiner and current government policies. This breadth of knowledge and understanding of Early Years enables graduates to articulate the rationales behind their practice with confidence. However, apart from different levels of academic qualifications, experience, continuing professional development and support through supervision, as discussed in Chapter 3, will also enable Key Persons to extend their knowledge and understanding of the needs of parents and their children, ensuring that each Key Person is provided with the skills to be able to build strong partnerships with parents.

McDowell Clark makes the point that:

> Building strong, reciprocal relationships requires respect and sensitivity on the part of practitioners and an inclusive ethos; conflicting values and beliefs are frequently reasons that parents do not access early years provision
>
> (McDowell Clark 2017 p. 75)

This quote, when analysed beside the situations in Reflection 1, Provocation 1 and the discussion points above related to outside influences, should provide you with the opportunity to reflect on your approach to parents/carers and the ways in which you show your respect and sensitivity to every parent with whom you communicate.

It is not suggested that this is an easy task! However, as with children, there are reasons for the behaviours and reactions exhibited by adults. Many of the reasons are listed above, but they may not be shared with you. When experiencing new situations or changes within family life it is often very difficult and very emotional for adults to share their problems and concerns. It is also very difficult if parents or carers have not experienced a good childhood themselves of if they feel that they are being judged or criticized for their values or beliefs, as explored in more depth in Chapter 5. They may feel that they are not respected and included. They may have very low self-esteem caused by many of those factors already mentioned. Nelson-Coffey et al. (2017), in a research paper related to attachment avoidance, highlight the importance of understanding parents' emotions during caregiving interactions because they have implications for parenting behaviours . . . parents' emotions are central to effective parenting.

(Dix 1991in Nelson-Coffey 2017 p. 505)

This quote is related to psychotherapy and the caregiving interactions between a parent and child. As Key Persons it is important to be aware that one person's emotional state can impact hugely on those around them and particularly on those closest to them. An acknowledgement of different emotions when you are working with parents and carers will help you to work sensitively and respectfully with parents and carers and to gradually gain their trust and respect. Now return to the beginning of this section and the factors identified at Pen Green as possible reasons for changes in behaviour.

You may find yourself in a situation where a parent is uncommunicative or aggressive. This can be hard work and even feel threatening. It is a time when supervision for Key Persons is required, see Chapter 3. However, although this is hard work, challenging and emotional, it can prove to be very rewarding for the Key Person and the other staff once you have gained the parents'/carers' trust and respect. The following case study illustrates the way that relationships can change when a parent is experiencing a time of stress in their own lives.

Case study 1

A member of staff, who was a Room Leader and Key Person for a child, asked for advice from the Day Care Manager. A parent who always appeared happy, very communicative, supportive, respectful and receptive when leaving and collecting an 18 month-old child had suddenly become very abrupt and tended to be rude. The member of staff was finding this very difficult to cope with and felt they must have done something wrong. The member of staff was reassured by the manager who suggested that there was, probably, a good reason for this assumed change in personality. The manager also said that they would ask to see the parent if the situation continued. However, only two mornings later, the parent asked the manager if they could speak with them. The parent acknowledged the fact that they had been rather aggressive but said they had been having medical tests and were awaiting the results. The results had now arrived. There was not a severe problem and already the parent was more relaxed and able to communicate. The parent apologised for passing their own stresses onto the member of staff. This was gently discussed and the manager suggested that, if able, the parent should apologise to the Room Leader too. The manager also said they would speak to the Room Leader to give reassurance. The situation was defused and the original strong partnership of mutual respect returned.

Points to consider having read through the case study:

- How was the member of staff feeling?

- What emotions would you experience in a similar situation?

- How would you manage your own emotions?

- How would you manage the situation?

- What impact might the possible loss of respect between the Key Person/Room Leader and the Parent have had on the child?

Mutual respect, which includes valuing parents/carers as their baby's or young child's first educator, will have an enormous impact on the very young child. He/she will become more settled because they too, feel safer and more secure when realizing their parent or carer is calmer and is accepted. You are building a strong, lasting partnership. However, should this mutual respect be compromised the child may become unsettled. Babies and very young children are very aware of changes in mood.

In relation to trusting and respecting parents and carers it must be remembered that, every minute of every day their child is learning. Learning does not just happen, as you know, in Early Years settings. Research has identified that babies and very young children learn through their environment (Bronfenbrenner 1979), the people they are with and the effects of different interactions and relationships through their daily routines and play experiences. Expressed simply through all of life's experiences, when at home babies and young children explore with their parents or carers who, generally, share their exploration and their feelings of awe, wonder and excitement. Sharing every one of a baby's or young child's new experiences through acknowledgement is reassuring for the baby/young child. Affirmation and acknowledgement help to build their self-confidence, often expressed in a wonderful smile from the baby or very young child. There are some instances where babies feel so pleased about receiving this affirmation that they experience a sense of 'chuffedness', feeling very proud of themselves, as described by Trevarthen (2003) and Arnold (2010). Their emotional needs are being met because they are being acknowledged. Here we are giving further consideration to the impact of the home as a learning environment, parents as a child's first educator and the link to babies' and children's emotional development.

To support the role of parents as first educators, we return to the following quote;

> Parenting has a bigger influence on a child's life chances in the early years than education, wealth or class
>
> (*State of the Nation* 2014)

Thus, the influence of parenting is given recognition and this recognition raises the parents'/carers' self-esteem, which in turn impacts on the self-esteem of their baby or young child. The knowledge that a parent has about their own child is vast, the parent is the *expert* (Ward 2016) and should be acknowledged, as stated above. However, children do react differently in different environments and with different people. There are times when a parent may not be able to speak about concerns they have about their baby or child and may deny having observed any areas of concern.

The names in the following case study have been changed.

Case study 2

Susie attended a day care setting from the age of four months. She had been born at full term and apparently had no problems. She was the youngest of three siblings, all females. Her home feeding, play and sleeping routine was closely followed and she appeared to settle into her new surroundings well and responded to her Key Person. However, from the beginning, her Key Person had some concerns about Susie's development. Susie had some difficulties with taking her bottle feeds in that she took a long time to feed, did not suck well and tended to dribble profusely. The problem was discussed with the room leader who suggested that the parent should be asked about the way Susie was fed at home – the way she was held, winded etc., followed by gentle questioning as to whether the parent had experienced any difficulties. The main answer was that 'No, there were no problems, all children are different', 'yes she takes longer to feed but that is not a problem.'

The explanation was accepted but at the same time concerns remained. Susie was gradually weaned following the routine provided by the parents, her routine for play and sleep was maintained but there were still concerns about her possible developmental delay. Parents and the Key Person exchanged information each morning and evening and at Parents' evenings but still the response was that 'all children are different.' Susie was making some progress, sitting, crawling and beginning to walk but each milestone was outside the expected norms. Her play provision was regularly discussed to ensure she was provided with appropriate resources that would encourage her all-round development. Her Key Person would play with her each day, one to one when many of the other children were resting. Susie's Parents were asked if Susie had been seen by the Health Visitor. 'Yes' but she has another appointment soon. The Manager asked the parent if it would be helpful for Susie's Key Person to contact the Health Visitor either before or after the appointment. It was decided that the Key Person should telephone the Health Visitor before the appointment and also provide a report on Susie's progress.

From this point on the parents, the Health Visitor, the Key Person and other professionals, as required, were able to work together to ensure Susie's individual care and developmental needs were being met through a strong partnership with everyone concerned, but particularly with the parents.

Having read this case study; what are/were your immediate thoughts? Why did the parents not acknowledge there was some developmental problem from the beginning?

It could be said that they were in denial. Why were they in denial?

This is one of the many challenges for professional Early Years Practitioners when you have identified a potential problem. Your knowledge and understanding of the needs and development of babies and young children provides you with the expertise to recognise when a child might not be progressing as they should. Conversely, the parent was absolutely right too, in that all children do develop at different rates and not always in the same order. Therefore, time had to be given to those parents so that they could recognise that there might be some delay. With the knowledge that 'early intervention' is key to ensuring each child reaches their full potential, as a professional it is hard not to be perhaps more direct at an earlier stage – a dilemma. Consider the fact that you want the parents to work with you, you do not want to alienate them because that would not have the desired outcome of supporting Susie's learning and development in partnership with her parents and other professionals. Susie was not in any form of danger and she was being supported both at home and in the setting, through observation, by responding to her individual learning and care needs and frequent, ongoing communication with her parents.

The journey to strong partnerships with parents in Early Years settings

When a young child starts attending an Early Years setting it marks the continuation of the journey through life for the young child and their family which obviously started with conception and the birth of the baby. Starting at an Early Years setting may be viewed as one of life's main events that involves varying degrees of stress for the parent/carer and baby or young child. The levels of stress are dependent on the way that this first transition is managed by the parent and Key Person. However, having made an initial visit to a setting and chosen the setting thought to be most suitable for the needs of the baby/young child and the family, the settling in period begins. The parents will have completed the required legal documentation such as the application form, information about their child and further information will be shared and recorded, for example on health problems, special needs, allergies, dietary requirements, routines, favourite toys, comforters, names of next of kin, those who may take the child to and from the setting, emergency contact names, email addresses and/or telephone numbers. If there are Child Protection issues, as you know, Social Services may be involved because the child might be on the 'At Risk Register' and there may be issues relating to access by certain adults.

The above administration all sounds very clinical and bureaucratic. However, it cannot be ignored, it is a legal requirement and without this information, as you know, you cannot begin to provide safety, care and education as a right for each child. You will already have shared basic information about the setting, the opening and closing, dropping off and collection times. You may have made a home visit which should help to establish the beginnings of the ensuing partnership with parents/carers. However, it is a time to be aware, mindful, of the fact that a parent or carer might feel that their home and their parenting skills are being inspected.

During the above meetings and contact times you will have continued to discuss the baby's or young child's individual needs whilst talking to the parent/carer and recording extra, helpful information that arises during these conversations and initial observations. Listening to and hearing has already been mentioned in this chapter. That is repeated here because listening and hearing should be reciprocal, that is, it is not simply that you should listen to and hear what the parent/carer has said/is saying but the parent/carer should also listen to and hear what you are saying. This is a challenge at times, especially when the parent/carer might be feeling nervous, but during these initial meetings, which are planned with time to talk and respond built in, you are able to provide the parent or carer with your undivided attention. Never be frightened about asking a parent or carer to repeat what they have said, or about repeating what you think they have said yourself. You are reaffirming what you have heard. Being able, as a Key Person, to give the parent and child your full attention, and demonstrate the respect and sensitivity required to establish a mutually respectful partnership should result in progression of the partnership. You will be able to acknowledge and refer to information that you have already received – listening, hearing, remembering and re-affirming.

You will ascertain from each parent/carer their expectations of the setting for their baby or young child. There will be varying expectations dependent upon the type of setting, whether large group, nursery or day care, or the smaller homely provision of a childminder. Even within each of these settings the provision will vary. Parents who choose to leave their baby/young child with a childminder are looking for home experiences. These home experiences can arouse anxieties for the parents/carers, perhaps about not experiencing interactions with other children of a similar age. Parents/carers may worry that the baby/young child could become too attached to their childminder or Key Person thus resulting in their baby/young child not maintaining the level of attachment to them as parent/carer. This was identified during the Baby Room Project by Goouch and Powell (2013) during discussions with baby room staff and by Elfer et al. (2003). Elfer et al. also speak about nursery, day care and preschool experiences as being different from home experiences, which they should be; however, *'they do need to fit together well.'* During experiences within Early Years settings, although different from home, babies and young children will be able to learn through interactions with their Key Person, other staff and children and, very importantly, the play opportunities provided that meet their individual needs, as discussed with their parents. They should fit together!

Reflection 3

How do you ensure that the experiences a child will be exposed to and enjoy, in your settings, fit in with the experiences a child is exposed to at home?

If, upon reflection, you think that they do not 'fit well together', how will you change your practice to ensure there is some harmony?

How will you manage the situation spoken about above, where a parent begins to feel that their baby is more attached to you as their Key Person?

The settling-in period

Early Years settings, as discussed in Chapter 3, will have a policy that allows for the differing needs of each child and their parents/carers. Thus, the process is not set in 'tablets of stone' but is flexible and adaptable. The settling-in period will be different for every parent or carer and every baby and young child although the policy and principles supporting the settling-in period should remain similar. You will experience different attitudes towards the settling-in process from parents/carers. There are those parents and carers who do not appreciate the value and importance of a gentle approach; they wish to transfer their baby or young child to the care of their Key Person and leave the setting immediately. This approach could be related to their own concerns about leaving; they do not want to be seen to be upset. They may appear to be uncaring and want to leave the setting as fast as they can, whilst other parents/carers just do not wish to leave. Separation, for them, is very hard but it could be argued that the parent who dashes away might be finding the experience of separation even harder.

Reflection 4

- Do you have a set policy for managing the settling-in period?

- How do you manage the situations when parents/carer feel very uncertain about leaving their baby/young child?

- Do you arrange times that fit in with the baby's/child's routine?

- How do you feel when, perhaps, the parents/carers are assertive about the time they are able to make the settling-in visits?

- How do you think the children and their parents/carers react to the approach that you adopt?

- Are you able to show respect and give both the children and their parents/carers the time and respect they deserve?

- Do they feel that you are rushing them?

- How calm and respectful are you?

Having reflected on these questions, how would you change your approach to ensure that you are calm and respectful and able to respond to the needs of each child and their parents/carers? Ask yourself how long the settling-in period should last?

Johnson (2016) included a reference to an ethos from one setting, presented by Marlen (2014) who spoke, during a conference, about 'A Gentle Beginning', and children needing time. She referred to the fact that Key Persons should be giving time for care routines to develop

> respectful care, good attachment, provided in a calm and peaceful manner.
>
> (Marlen 2014)

The implementation of *tactful, respectful care* is one of the elements of the Pikler Approach. She also believed that babies and young children should have complete freedom of movement, freedom to explore.

> The application of Emmi Pikler's respectful and affectionate image of the baby, to various contexts of care around the world (day care, institutions, families) approach [sic], has helped babies to develop well, and adults to change their internal representations of the baby's capacities and their role as care providers.
>
> (Tardos 2010 p. 4)

Emmi Pikler trained as a paediatrician and set up a nursery home for infants in Budapest, Hungary in1946 for homeless infants. This home later became known as the Pikler Institute and is still open today (Tardos 2010).

> [H]er vision of a healthy infant was an active, competent and peaceful infant, who lives in peace with himself and his environment.
>
> (Tardos 2010 p. 1)

Lumsden (2014), during the same Conference, also spoke about the fact that all children need time and space to play and to experience quality play because, 'every interaction counts', and the best qualified staff reflect first before reacting (Perkins 2014 in Johnson 2016 pp. 236–237).

The above quotes were from presentations heard during a conference organised by the organisation, 'What about the Children', in 2014. It was very thought-provoking and, as can be read above, related closely to the emotional needs of very young children and their all-round development. The strong message that children need to be given time and respectful care was so powerful and is thought to be very true. The settling-in period for the children in the setting referred to by Marlen was as long as was necessary for the baby/child. Parents/carers were allowed to stay as long as they wished, with times for short trial separations when the parent/carer remained on the premises. This approach enabled the baby/child to begin to understand that their parent/carer would return.

Consider the age when many babies begin to attend an Early Years setting. It is often between the ages of nine months and one year because these are the ages at which maternity allowances come to an end and Mothers have to make a decision about extending their maternity leave to one year or returning to work when their baby is nine months old. This is at a time in a baby's development when the baby has developed a strong attachment to the Mother but when he/she does not understand that although the parent/carer is not there, they do still exist. Piaget carried out experiments by hiding objects under a blanket for a baby of between six and seven months to find. It was not until approximately eight to ten months of age that a baby would look for the object under the blanket. Piaget termed this, as most of you will know, 'object permanence.' Therefore, this can prove to be a difficult time for babies to start attending Early Years settings. Each baby needs the time, respectful care and opportunity for a good attachment to be provided by a calm Key Person.

On reflection, these quotes and the dates when they first originated, cover over 70 years up until the present day. However, that is a relatively short period of time in comparison with the fact that the concept of responding to the individual needs of children, to enable them to move around freely and to explore and for Early Years Practitioners and teachers to follow the interests of the child has been addressed by Early Years pioneers, researchers and professionals for hundreds of years, for example by Comenius (1592–1670) who stated that,

> 'Teachers ought to "follow in the footsteps of nature," meaning that they ought to pay attention to the mind of the child and to the way the student learned.
>
> (John E Sadler undated)

Jean Jacques Rousseau (1762) subsequently recognised the importance of the Early Years and saw education as a gift learned *'from nature, from men and from things'* p. 1. Friedrich Froebel (1782–1852), Susan Isaacs (1885–1948), Margaret Donaldson (1926-), Maria Montessori (1870–1952) and Rudolph Steiner

(1861–1925) promoted the use and value of observation and outdoor play and of following the interests of the child. Thus, the message to observe and then provide children with the freedom to explore and play remains the same. The values of play and outdoor play are still being debated and researched today by Moyles, Fisher and especially by Bruce who has many publications about play, and recently, with others, has updated the Froebel approach to Early Childhood Practice (2012). Tovey (2008) and Solly (2015) value and research outdoor play, with the freedom but risk and challenge that it presents. Both authors present strong evidence of the benefits of outdoor play which link to the Pikler principle that children should be free to move and explore. It is this freedom of movement that should be explored in more detail. The concept of the need for continuous movement is also linked to learning and development, not just physical development but also neuroscience, by Goddard Blythe (2005), who speaks about the immediate cell division following conception which can be observed as constant movement. She sees movement as imperative for children's learning.

> Just as the brain controls the body, the body has much to teach the brain
>
> (Goddard Blythe 2005 p. 3)

If, in your settings you respect the need for children to experience a gentle, calm settling-in period where you provide resources that meet the interests of the baby or young child while enabling them room and time to explore, you will also be responding to their emotional needs and working with parents and carers to ensure the babies and young children settle well. You are developing a strong, trusting relationship with the parents or carers and their children.

Maintaining a strong, trusting partnership with parents

Having managed a successful settling-in period for a baby or young child and built a partnership with their parents or carers that shows obvious signs of mutual respect, it is now important to maintain and build upon this relationship. Good, continuous communication is a key to achieving a lasting partnership. There are many forms of communication that have developed rapidly over the last 50 years. In the past, communication was relatively slow, via mail, or telephone (land lines only and not every household had or has a landline). Now nearly every adult has a mobile phone, a computer and/or a tablet. We have the facility for immediate communication with texts, emails, social media and via the internet. Children's records in Early Years settings and schools can be accessed by their parents via apps such as Tapestry where information can be exchanged between parents/carers and the setting their baby/child attends. Parents are encouraged to upload and share photographs of and information about activities the children may have been involved in over a weekend, a holiday or special occasion.

The point that texts and emails are remote could be discussed and analysed in that there is no personal contact but, conversely, this form of contact or communication is better than no communication at all. A thought – can electronic communication completely replace one to one personal communication? What a thought!! Whilst acknowledging the requirement for using modern forms of communication it remains so important that safe websites and apps are used with secure passwords, as you are all aware. Care must be taken with the written word too, meaning emails. A quick email sent in the heat of the moment, without careful thought, can undermine positive relationships in a second.

Electronic communication does have its place and in the busy lives of most parents and carers it does result in improved levels of information being passed between Early Years settings and parents or carers.

Reflection 5

Reflect on an occasion when you might have received an email that contained upsetting content.

▪ How did it make you feel?

▪ What prompted the email?

▪ How did you deal with the problem?

▪ Have you ever sent an email that upset the recipient and how did you manage the ensuing difficulties?

Having reflected on this situation, identified a time when you received an email you were unhappy about and thought about the way you managed the event. What strategies did you put in place to try to avoid such a situation in the future? Did you/do you have a policy for emailing parents or using electronic forms of communication? Have you changed your practices?

Concerns that parents may share

Earlier in this chapter some of the challenges that parents and Key Persons may face together were identified. These challenges were mainly related to the factors that can prevent parents from becoming involved with the care and education of their baby or young child. The different forms of childcare provision have been considered along with the impact of government initiatives such as the 30 hours of free childcare for three to four year-old children. However, there are many more concerns or expectations that parents may express. These concerns and expectations are fuelled partly through articles spread via social media and partly through articles published in the national press or reported on the news. They can also be fuelled during conversations between parents

Consider the following provocation.

Provocation I

You are working in a day care setting where you provide for the care, individual interests and learning needs of children who are aged from three months to five years. The setting follows the Early Years Foundation Stage (2017) framework with a strong focus on outdoor provision, making use of a large, secure open area surrounded by some woodland – wonderful for exploration. The children spend most of their time outside, fully supervised. They are climbing, exploring, finding minibeasts, digging, jumping in puddles, scooting, creating dens, problem solving and having an amazing time. They are learning so much from nature, one could say they are at one with nature. However, a parent comes to see you because they are not happy about the level of maths and literacy their child is experiencing because they have heard that their child, aged four, should be preparing for, made ready for, school. The parent has heard that their child should be able to read short sentences, use phonics to read out new words, write short sentences using phonics to spell the words (EYFS 2017). They should also be able to count from 1–20, add and subtract in ones or twos, speak about more and less, bigger and smaller, know shapes, weights and measures. The parent becomes quite indignant stating, 'I don't think that sort of learning is going on here. I've downloaded the EYFS and can see what you should be teaching.'

This provocation has been chosen deliberately because it is an ongoing dilemma for parents and Key Persons that is so often debated. Given the pressure for all children to achieve and given the fact that all parents want the best for their children, parents do keep raising this issue because they are led to believe that is very important for children to begin to achieve the skills of reading and writing from the age of five years. This is despite research from the Netherlands, France, Spain and other countries in Europe where formal schooling does not commence until children are at least six years of age and in some instances, for example in Eastern Europe, children are seven years of age before starting formal schooling. The children are allowed to play, to learn to count through games that involve counting and size, problem solving, new words, listening to the sounds of nature and describing them together. There are no pencils and paper in that outdoor area but there are never ending natural resources. In England the statutory age for starting school is just five and it is possible to enter school at only four years of age. Parents are often heard to say that they don't really want their child to start school when he/she is just four 'but if we don't take the place we will probably lose it.' Think about the advice you might give a parent in this situation.

If you work in a setting that provides wonderful outdoor play, how will you work with the parent to reassure them that their child is learning through the amazing daily outdoor experiences provided in this setting? Are you able to fully articulate the learning that is taking place and that all areas of learning are included? What are the experiences that will assist them, when they are ready, to hold a pencil and ultimately to write? How will you promote children's fine manipulative skills in the outdoor area?

You have been left with several questions that are intended to help you to continue to reflect on your practice, to ensure that you do question, assess and then develop strategies that will enable you to work with and to form informed, respectful partnerships with the parents and carers in your settings.

Conclusion

The theme throughout this chapter has been 'Working in partnership with parents' to ensure that the individual care and learning needs of the children who attend your settings are met. The priority has remained the emotional needs of the children because, as stated throughout this book, if a child does not feel safe, secure, valued and respected, i.e. their emotional needs are not met, he/she will not be able to learn to their full potential. The emotional needs of very young children are inherently linked to the emotions and past experiences of their parents, as identified at the beginning of this chapter. They are, but do remember that these possible barriers can gradually be overcome if you form a reciprocal, sensitive, respectful partnership with parents where a sense of trust has been developed and maintained.

Consideration has also been given to the impact of external sources, government initiatives, papers and legislation that affect choices of childcare and educational settings. The impact of good parenting on children's successes throughout life and the detrimental effects of poverty have been included (State of the Nation 2014). The importance of the home learning environment and the parent as the expert have been addressed. The case studies, reflections and provocations have helped you to consider your own practice when working with parents and to develop new strategies that help both you as Key Persons and the parents or carers. The importance of forming reciprocal, sensitive relationships with parents and/or carers has been stressed again in this conclusion and throughout the chapter. Links have been made to the Early Years pioneers who, for hundreds of years, have recognised the importance of the early years, of observation and working with families and their communities. Therefore, your deepening knowledge and understanding of the needs of very young children both from a historic perspective and from practice today, along with the needs of their parents will help you to form strong informed partnerships with parents. All of the above endorse the importance of the role of the Key Person in forming a very positive relationship with parents or first carers.

Further reading

State of the Nation Reports – 2014 and 2015 Social Mobility and Child Poverty in Great Britain

> We should not tolerate early years services that do not prepare children for school.
> 'The life chances of children, the poorest especially, depend on many things including good parenting, childcare, education and employment.
> Child Poverty Act 2010 and Welfare Reform Act 2012

McDowall Clark, R (2017) Exploring the Contexts for Early Learning – Challenging the School Readiness Agenda, Oxon: Routledge.
The Child Poverty Act 2010, the Welfare Reform Act 2012 and the State of the Nations Reports provide strong support for and evidence of the effects of poverty on children's life chances. It is suggested that you use these documents, and the book by McDowall Clark, to discuss the two quotes above in relation to your work with parents and their children. There have been many debates about the concept of school readiness and exactly how it is interpreted. What is your interpretation of the term and is it a term you use with parents?

Barlow, J; Svanberg, P O (2010) *Keeping the Baby in Mind Infant Mental Health Practice*, Routledge: East Sussex.
This entire text will provide you with in-depth knowledge about the importance of working with parents and helping those requiring extra support to respond sensitively and appropriately to their babies and very young children. There is also information about mind-mindedness which is the ability of a 'mother to interpret her baby's feelings. The better the baby's intentions and mood are interpreted the faster he or she is able to represent their thoughts and feelings through language and play' (p. 5). Topics directly related to those introduced and discussed in this chapter include:

- Keeping the baby in mind

- The power of touch – infant baby massage

- Promoting the early parent-infant relationship

- Empowering parents through 'Learning together'

- Mellow Babies – mellow parenting with parents of infants

- Developing infant-centred services

- Working with the hidden obstacle in parent-infant relating.

Empowering parents through 'Learning together' has also been recommended as further reading for Chapter 2 on attachment. It expands the information on the Peers Early Education Partnership (PEEP) you may already have read about in the chapter, 'Keeping the baby in mind,' and is pertinent to your work with parents and carers in your settings.

References

Arnold, C (2010) Understanding Schemas and Emotion in Early Childhood, London: Sage

Barlow, J; Svanberg, P O (2009) *Keeping the Baby in Mind Infant Mental Health Practice*, Routledge: East Sussex

Bowlby, J (1969/1991) 2nd Ed *Attachment and Loss: Volume1, Attachment*, London: Penguin

Bruce, T (Ed) (2012) *Early Childhood Practice – Froebel Today*, London: Sage Publications

Child Poverty Act 2010 www.legislation.gov.uk/ukpga/2010/9/contents accessed 23 February 2018

DoE (2017) *The Early Years Foundation Stage Framework*, UK: DoE https://www.gov.uk/.../early-years-foundation-stage-profile-handbook accessed 23 February 2018

DofE (2016) *An Early Years National Funding Formula*, UK: DofE accessed 11 October 2017

Donaldson, M (1978) *Children's Minds*, London: Fontana Press

Dowling, M (2010) 3rd Ed Young Children's Personal, Social and Emotional Development, London: Paul Chapman

Elfer, P; Goldschmied, E; Selleck, D (2003) *Key Persons in the Nursery*, London: David Fulton

Fonagy, P (2003) The development of psychopathology from infancy to adulthood: the mysterious unfolding of disturbance in time', *In Infant Mental Health Journal*, 24 (3): 212–239. May 2003, accessed 10 April 2017

Georgeson, J; Payler, J (2013) International Perspectives on Early Childhood Education and Care, Maidenhead: OU Press

Goddard Blythe, S (2005) *The Well Balanced Child*, Gloucestershire: Hawthorn Press

Goouch, K and Powell, S (2013) *The Baby Room*, Berkshire: Oxford University Press

HMSO (2014) *The State of the Nation – Social Mobility and Child Poverty Commission* www.gov.uk/government accessed 23 February 2018

House of Commons Library (2017) *Funding for Maintained Nursery Schools 2017* UK:Gov www.researchbriefings.files.parliament.uk/fundingformaintainednurseryschools/debatepackfor01Feb2017/CDP-2017-0033/30Jan2017 accessed 23 February 2018

Jarrett, T and Perks, D (2017) *Funding for Maintained Nursery Schools* http://research-briefings.parliament.uk/ResearchBriefing/Summary/CDP-2017-0033 accessed 1 March 2018

Johnson, T (2016) Holistic Development: The Social and Emotional Needs of Children, in *The Early Years Handbook for Students and Practitioners*, Ed. Trodd, L, Oxon: Routledge

Marlen, D (March 2014) *A Gentle Beginning*, presented to the Royal Overseas League.

McDowell Clark, R (2017) *Exploring the Contexts for Early Learning*, Abingdon: Routledge

Nelson-Coffey, S K; Borelli, J; River, L M; (2017) Attachment avoidance, but not anxiety, minimizes the joys of caregiving in *Attachment and Human Development Journal* 19, (5): 504–531, Oxon: Routledge

Nursery World 11 August 2016 https://www.nurseryworld.co.uk/nursery-world/news/1158
588/sector-response-early-years-national-funding-formula accessed 20 October 2017

Nutbrown, C (2012) *Foundations for Quality, The Independent Review of Early Education
and Childcare Qualifications*, London: DfE

Rousseau, J J (1762) *Emile – translation by Barbara Foxley*, Great Britain: Amazon

Solly, K (2015) *Risk, Challenge and Adventure in the Early Years*, Oxon: Routledge

Sadler, J E (undated) *Comenius* https://www.britannica.com/biography/John-Amos-
Comenius) accessed 3 November 2017

Tardos, A (2010) Introducing the Piklerian developmental approach: History and principles
pp. 1–4: *The Signal*, International Association for Infant Mental Health Jul – Dec 2010
USA www.waimh.org/files, accessed 20 September 2017

Tovey, H (2008) Playing Outdoors – Spaces and Places, Risk and Challenge, Maidenhead:
McGraw Hill.

Trevarthen, C (2003) *Chuffedness – the Motor of Learning*, Pen Green Conference, June 2003

UK Welfare Reform Act 2012 www.legislation.gov.uk/ukpga/2012/5/contents/enacted
accessed 23 February 2018

Ward, U (2016) The Child Family and Society: Working in Partnership with Parents, in *The
Early Years Handbook for Students and Practitioners*, Ed. Trodd, L; Oxon: Routledge

Whalley, M (2001) *Involving Parents in their Children's Learning*, London: Paul Chapman
Publishing Ltd

Website

file:///C:/ INetCache/IE/H9I0XYFR/Summary_State_of_the_Nation_2014.pdf accessed 14
October 2016

5 The effects of different cultures experienced by very young children

Key themes in this chapter

After reading this chapter you should be able to:

- Articulate the meaning of the word 'culture' in many of its guises

- Consider the different cultures experienced in your settings

- Analyse the impact of different cultures on your settings, the children attending, the staff and the environment

- Analyse and critique the impact of the culture in your setting on the children who attend

- Analyse the culture of learning in your setting

- Reflect on and adapt your practice to include the various cultures that are brought into your settings

- Analyse and critique culture in relation to language and cultural practices, recent research and the Early Years Foundation Stage.

Introduction

Human beings have a special kind of intelligence with a capacity for sympathy of brain activity that drives learning of what the society values and what the culture has made.

(Trevarthen (2004 p. 1)

The natural creativity and cooperation of infants and toddlers, their self-produced motives for acting and knowing with other people, are given less attention than their needs for care and protection. They are perceived to require instruction in skills of moving, speaking, reasoning and behaving well socially.

(Trevarthen 2011 p. 175)

The above quotes from Trevarthen (2004) and (2011), whilst being used to introduce forms of culture and attitudes to culture, also create links to each of the chapters in this book. In the paper, Making Friends with Infants, presented at a Conference in Pen Green in 2004, he spoke about feelings of triumph and failure, the effects of deprivation and inadequate parenting, as well as the neurological effects on the development of the brain if a child is experiencing stress and insecure attachment, each point relating to the emotional needs of very young children, already explored and discussed in Chapters 1 to 4 in this book. The quotes from Trevarthen (2011) support the need for babies and young children to learn a culture but also identify their ability and desire to learn with others about their culture, to be a part of a community. Throughout this chapter references are made to the preceding chapters because of the way that all experiences influence everyday life and our cultures.

Consideration is given to the immediate cultures experienced by children, the culture of their home, their extended families, the culture within the setting or settings they may attend and the impact of different cultural experiences that Early Years Practitioners may bring to the setting. The concept of mindfulness is introduced in relation to, 'paying more attention to the present moment – to your own thoughts and feelings, and the world around you' (NHS 2016). Therefore, not only the effects of cultures but moods, health, expectations etc are considered. International perspectives are included when referring to the different cultures within childcare provision.

Culture, in its various forms, is all around us. However, before addressing culture linked specifically to children during their early years and the different cultures that are encountered in Early Years settings it is important for you to consider the meanings of the word culture. The following definitions of culture from a *Dictionary of Psychology* (1995), *The Concise Oxford Dictionary* (1995) and from Haralambos and Holborn (2000), in their book *Sociology, Themes and Perspectives* provide an introduction to the concept of culture. These definitions are included as points of reference and points for discussion, critique and reflection. They have also been chosen to help you to maintain a focus on the meanings of the word whilst exploring the different forms of culture that exist not only within the Early Years but in our day to day lives and society as a whole.

What is culture?

Culture is:

1. *The system of information that codes the manner in which the people in an organised group, society or nation interact with their social and physical environment. In this sense the term is really used so that the frame of reference is the sets of rules, regulations, mores and methods of interaction within the group. A key connotation is that culture pertains only to non-genetically given transmission: each member must learn the systems and the structures.*

2. *The group or collection of persons who share the patterned systems described in 1.*

Reber 1995 p. 177

Mores are social norms and customs that provide the moral standards of behaviour of a group or society. They refer to social customs rather than formally enacted laws.

(Reber 1995 p. 470)

In contrast to the above definitions which are related to psychology and, perhaps, are gentler and more fitting when considering culture in relation to the Early Years, the following definitions from the Concise Oxford Dictionary provide shorter, concise definitions of culture:

1a. the arts and other manifestations of human intellectual achievement regarded collectively (a city lacking in culture)

1b. a refined understanding of this; intellectual development (a person of culture)

2. The customs, civilisation, and achievements of a particular time or people.

3. Improvement by mental or physical training

(Concise Oxford Dictionary 9th Ed 1995 p. 328)

These definitions from the Concise Oxford Dictionary relate to human customs and achievements, from group achievement, such as a city, to the refined individual understanding of each person, a person of culture, as stated above.

Haralambos and Holborn (2000) speak about culture as being very difficult to define because there are so many variations in people's understanding and interpretation of culture. They also speak about the helplessness of a new born baby and the need for each baby to 'learn the culture of its society.' Trevarthen (2005) provided an insight into the speed with which learning begins to take place for a newly born infant, 'the baby can feel its own body and within minutes can relate to objects outside its body,' and when only '30 minutes old a baby begins imitating facial expressions.' A baby is beginning to communicate and, through this interaction with a responsive adult, is already at the very, very early stages of beginning to learn about his or her culture, initially his or her immediate culture within the home.

Piaget's interpretation of culture in some respects supports the views of Trevarthen, in that he considered that a baby was continuously influenced by the surrounding environment from birth.

> The human being is immersed right from birth in a social environment which affects him just as much as his physical environment. Society, even more, in a sense, than the physical environment, changes the very structure of the individual . . . Every relation between individuals (from two onwards) literally modifies them.
>
> (Piaget, 1950, reprinted 2002, pp. 171–172; also cited by Woodhead 1998 p. 14)

Linton (1945) described the culture of a society as, 'the way of life of its members; the collection of ideas and habits which they learn, share and transmit from generation to generation.' (Cited by Haralambos and Holborn (2000) p. viii).

Haralambos and Holborn (2000) speak about behaviour within cultures being based on 'guidelines that are learned' and say that they must be 'shared by its members.' These are described as 'qualities of culture.' Within each culture or group of society each baby and very young child begins to learn 'a sense of self', they develop their own identity. Frosh (1999) stated that,

> a person's identity is multiple and fluid . . . constructed through experience and linguistically coded. People draw on culturally available resources in their immediate social networks and society as a whole.
>
> (Cited in Haralambos and Holborn 2000, p. 793)

Links to nature, planting and growing crops of vegetables and flowers, are often cited as an interpretation of culture, for example Woodhead said, following on from Tyler's definition of culture as

> that complex whole which includes knowledge, belief, art, morals, law, custom, and any other capabilities and habits acquired by man as a member of society.
>
> (Tyler (1874) cited in Woodhead 1998 p. 15)

A garden as an artificial-environment-for-growing-things is a complex whole, and gardening requires knowledge, beliefs, and the like, as an integral part of the process.

> (Woodhead 1998 p. 15)

Given the complexity of the term culture and the subdivisions of culture presented in the definitions above, it is suggested that you return to the introductory quotes by Trevarthen at the beginning of this chapter.

Reflection I

Re-read and reflect on the each of the quotes from Trevarthen:

- What were your initial thoughts when you first read the quote?

- What were your thoughts when reading the dictionary definitions?

- Have your thoughts and ideas about culture changed now that you have considered the quote from Trevarthen, the definitions from the Dictionary of Psychology and the Concise Oxford Dictionary?

- Which definitions support your own ideas about culture?

- Can culture be further subdivided?

When reading the introduction and the definitions of culture you will have had many thoughts in your mind about different cultures. If culture is considered in its broadest sense, there is the culture of humanity, the overall society of the world. 'However, you might immediately be thinking, 'but how can we consider humanity as one culture?' 'How can we consider the life of peoples in different parts of the world sharing the same values and societies that we experience?' In many respects we cannot, because they don't, but if we consider Maslow's hierarchy of need we all have the same basic needs to enable us to survive and to achieve. Basically, all human beings need food, water, love, shelter, warmth, to be valued, to develop a sense of self-esteem and to achieve. Cole (1998) discusses an 'emphasis of culture as a difference.' He says that:

> it overlooks the fact that the capacity to inhabit a culturally organized environment is universal, a species-specific characteristic of homo sapiens.
>
> (Cole 1998 p. 11)

It is interesting to read that the subject of culture has usually been approached in a way that identified cultural differences, often with an interpretation of a deficit model. Do you consider, when reading about Early Years provision, researching for comparisons of different curricula, that this continues to be the approach today? Do the statements by Cole and Trevarthen support the suggestion that there is a culture within the whole of humanity, as stated above?

We are influenced and have been influenced by our immediate culture, family culture, our environment, those around us in Early Years settings, schools, clubs, workplaces, and cultures experienced through travel, the media of television and social media such as Facebook, Twitter and through advertising. However, before moving onto the evolving culture within the twenty-first century that affects our lifestyles, Early Years provision, education, fashion, sport and such things as holidays and leisure time the impact of our history and migration are briefly considered.

Today, we in the United Kingdom live in a multi-cultural society and have done for thousands of years, as Siraj-Blatchford (2010) says, making the point that,

> We have never been a monocultural society.
>
> (Siraj-Blatchford 2010 p. 154)

The fact that we have been multicultural for thousands of years has also been discovered during many archaeological digs, such as during the construction of the new Crossrail in London, where the remains of bodies have been found in mass graves beneath Liverpool Street Station, London.

> Since Crossrail construction began in 2009, more than 10,000 archaeology items, spanning more than 55 million years of London's history, have been found across over 40 construction sites.
>
> (Heritage Daily.com 2013/10)

Given these finds, many of which are now on display in the Docklands Museum, they provide evidence of forms of life and different civilisations existing where London now stands, as it states above, spanning more than 55 million years. This is difficult to comprehend in some respects. However, the point being made concerns the multicultural nature of most societies. Migration has occurred throughout the centuries resulting, as you know, in cultures changing and evolving. Archaeological sites such as Stonehenge and Avebury Rings, plus structures like the Roman Baths in Bath and the Roman Roads, such as Fosse Way, Ermine Street ad Watling Street (built to improve military and commercial access between major towns) continue to provide evidence of changing cultures. The changes in culture were/are often due to invasion and migration.

Reasons for migration

What has caused migration in the past and what is causing migration now? There are many, usually external, influences that result in changes to our cultures and societies and cause people to migrate. In past and present times people have migrated at different times of the year in order to survive. These people were/are nomadic; they moved/move to areas where crops grew well so that they could to feed themselves and their animals. Sometimes this migration was seasonal. They were often trying to ensure their survival by escaping the excessive heat of summer or the intense freezing cold of winter. Much migration takes place, as we are too aware, in times of conflict, when people wish to keep themselves and their families safe.

They are searching, perhaps, for a 'better life.' Joining relatives who have already migrated, they may be fleeing wars, persecution and local conflicts, injury and often death. Whilst they will be entering a new culture in the area/country to which they migrate, this new culture may have a profound effect on the immigrants and their way of life. They will, however, bring aspects of their own culture with them which may impact on their new local community. The reasons for migration considered here have been linked to migration from one country to another. However, moving within the United Kingdom can be considered as migration. Each country and areas within that country will have different cultures and values. This is particularly noticeable in the United Kingdom which, as you know consists of England, Northern Ireland, Scotland and Wales. On the national and local news, we frequently hear about the effects that Brexit may have, especially for Ireland, Gibraltar and British Overseas Territories, and there is also the north/south divide within England. The north/south divide is linked to the economy, poverty, educational experiences and examination results, employment, and differences in opportunities for those living in towns and rural areas.

Living and working in a multicultural society

So far, this chapter has explored the meaning of the word 'culture' and applied the word culture to our changing societies in a broad global sense, both historic and in the present time. It has also encouraged you to begin to think, in more depth, about the cultures around you and to raise awareness of some of the causes of the ever-changing cultures in our immediate society today. Your thoughts will now be re-directed towards your role in Early Years and the support that you may provide for children from many different cultures who may attend your settings.

Reflection 2

Reflect on the number of children who attend your settings:

- Are all of the children from your local area?

- How many of the children have always lived in the area?

- Do you have children who have recently moved to the area?

- Do you have children for whom English is their second language?

- Do the children's parents speak English?

- How do you ensure that all children and their parents feel welcomed and valued?

- Think of an incident when a child and their parents did not settle into your environment.

  - How did you manage the situation?

  - What would you change so that you could manage the situation differently and more effectively in future?

This reflection is very closely linked to your role as a Key Person, addressed in more detail in both Chapters 3 (Key Persons) and 4 (Working with Parents). However, here the focus is 'the culture' and 'the cultural needs of children and their families' including acknowledgment of the many global issues that have already been identified in this chapter. Also, keep in mind the fact that all children and adults have the propensity and ability to learn a culture and are generally able to adapt to different cultures. Elfer et al. (2003) offer a table giving examples from some of the standards within the 2001 National Standards of Care – Standards 3, Care Learning and Play; 8, Food and Drink; and 9, Equal Opportunities. The subject of culture was recorded in these three standards alone and referred narrowly to:

Standard 3 – Children will be communicating and playing in the home languages as well as in English. Key Persons will value this development and will know about the cultural identities, languages and religions of each child and his/her family.

Standard 8 – The Key Person will ensure the food and the methods of eating it are congruent with the cultural traditions of the families and staff in each setting/group.

Standard 9 – The Key Person will ensure that some of the books, toys, play materials, labels and displays value the racial origin, religion, language and culture of the child's family.

Whilst the Early Years Foundation Stage Framework Profile 2017 (Standards and Testing Agency 2016) does not mention culture specifically, it is implicit in:

Equality of opportunity and **anti-discriminatory practice**, ensuring that every child is included and supported (p. 5)

1.5 **Understanding the world** involves guiding children to make sense of their physical world and their community through opportunities to explore, observe and find out about people, places, technology and the environment.

1.7 For children whose home language is not English, providers must take reasonable steps to provide opportunities for children to develop and use their home language in play and learning, supporting their language development at home.

If a child does not have a strong grasp of English language, practitioners must explore the child's skills in the home language with parents and/or carers, to establish whether there is cause for concern about language delay.

1.8 Practitioners must respond to each child's emerging needs and interests, guiding their development through warm, positive interaction. (p. 8)

The specific areas:

People and communities: children talk about past and present events in their own lives and in the lives of family members. They know that other children don't always enjoy the same things, and are sensitive to this. They know about similarities and differences between themselves and others, and among families, communities and traditions.

The world: children know about similarities and differences in relation to places, objects, materials and living things. They talk about the features of their own immediate environment and how environments might vary from one another. They make observations of animals and plants and explain why some things occur, and talk about changes. (p. 12).

The above selections from the EYFS (2017) have been included because, as stated above, the subject of culture is implicit rather than explicit. Compare and contrast the two different approaches to the inclusion of culture and critique the management of cultural needs within your settings. Do you consider that National Standards of Care provide the Practitioner with more direct information and guidance or does the EYFS provide sufficient information and guidance? Could it be said that given the length of time between the publication of the National Standards of Care in 2001 and the EYFS in 2017, society in England has become more aware of multicultural society and of responding to the emotional and cultural needs of each child. As the EYFS states, *every child is a unique child.*

Moving on from migration from one country to another country, Thomas (2017) researched the need for support for adults and children when they move house within their own country, particularly when they move into a different area, away from extended family. Every family or household, has its own culture, as does every Early Years setting, every school, every town or village and every organisation within that town or village. Earlier in the chapter you were asked if culture can be subdivided, the question has been answered, in part, throughout this chapter so far and immediately above. When considering moving within one's own country we have moved through a set of micro-cultures to the larger cultures of the local areas. Moving house, changing Early Years settings and schools are known as 'major life events'; they are difficult times, even though, in the majority of instances, the moves are being made for positive reasons. BUT the immediate, familiar support has temporarily been taken away and replaced with uncertainty.

Reflection 3

Identify an event in your lives when you have felt very insecure:

■ Reflect on the event and the reasons for your insecurity

■ How did you feel?

■ Why did you feel this way?

■ What could have alleviated your insecurity or other feelings?

■ How could you use this experience to help the children and families in your settings?

■ Given the opportunity for this reflection what changes could you make to your practice?

The significance of culture and identity

A culture generally provides the members of a society or group with sets of beliefs, rules, regulations, language, expected social norms, customs, rituals, values and ways of interacting with each other and conforming. Trevarthen (1998) sees being part of a culture 'as a need human-beings are born with'. Initially this need is addressed within the home environment, the culture of the home, where there are varying sizes of family group. MacDougall and Brown describe this as the

> cultural, geographical and socio-economic environment of their parents or carers' who will 'shape the lives of their very young child
>
> (MacDougall and Brown 2016 p. 104.)

Earlier in the chapter the various cultures within the larger cultural groups have been referred to as 'micro-cultures.' In the micro-culture of the home, not only is a very young child's life shaped, but it is through this culture that he or she begins to learn their own identity in relation to that culture. We will presume, for the moment, that there is continuation of the development of self-identity when a very young child is exposed to external environments and cultures outside the home environment because it will emulate relatively closely the culture that has been experienced within their own home. That is, the beliefs, rules, language, social norms, customs and values are similar. However, as already stated, they will not be exactly the same because no two people interpret aspects of culture in exactly the same way, although there is usually a consensus of opinion in relation to cultural expectations and norms. Remember, not only is each child unique, so is each person on planet Earth. Below is a provocation that has been included as an illustration of different interpretations and describes a very familiar situation.

Provocation I

Consider the advice given to the Mother of a newborn infant – how confusing it is because, very often, everyone gives slightly different or conflicting advice. How does or should the Mother manage this advice? It can be very difficult for her, she may still be getting to know her baby, what its cries mean and how to handle this very tiny person. The advice may be given by the baby's grandmother to the Mother; it could be termed culturally acceptable as it is being handed down from generation to generation. However, given that there are always changes in the advice provided by the media, midwives, health visitors and doctors, advice from the grandmother might be challenged by the baby's Mother, who may be feeling confused and anxious.

This provocation is included to illustrate the very small differences in culture that may exist within the extended family. It also alludes to the fact that practices change. Imagine the above situation. Whilst being a very happy time, the birth of a baby can also be quite stressful. How will a baby learn its identity if the Mother is stressed?

As already stated above, Trevarthen writes about a baby beginning to learn a culture almost immediately it is born. The baby begins to recognise faces and facial expressions that it can imitate and which the adult can repeat. The baby is being responded to, being acknowledged through the expressions. The Mother or carer will also be talking quietly to the baby, who in turn will be smiling and then gradually beginning to reply to the Mother or carer with gurgles and coos. Trevarthen termed these verbal interactions 'proto-conversations.' Proto-conversations were also discussed in Chapter 2, in relation to attachment. It is through these interactions that the baby is beginning to learn about his or her surroundings, the noises, the language and music, their care, their siblings and their culture.

Changing cultures within the home and the environment

Whilst a baby begins to learn a culture almost immediately he or she is born, the perinatal period should be taken into consideration too. When in utero, as has been discussed before in Chapter 2, a baby is able to hear. Pinker (1995) affirms that babies are able to hear when in the uterus and that babies are already able to recognise their Mother's language. If the language they have heard is French they respond to French but not to English or Italian. Trevarthen has spoken about a baby being eager to communicate, to participate in proto-conversations and enjoying music, particularly that associated with the culture into which he or she has been born. Chomsky considered that human beings have a language acquisition device, whilst Pinker (1995) spoke about the language instinct and the new science of language and mind, both inferring that babies are tuned-in to learning a language.

Neuroscience continues to provide evidence and support for previous findings, as mentioned above, that during the perinatal period, the sounds the baby is exposed to in utero, although muffled due to the sound waves having to pass through the Mother's abdominal wall, the uterine wall, the placenta and the amniotic fluid, are already providing information to the baby about his or her cultural world. These sounds will include language, music, traffic, the sounds within the Mother's abdominal cavity. In fact, it has been evidenced already that a baby is soothed by the Mother's voice and certain music that he or she heard whilst in utero. Recordings of the sounds heard by the baby whilst in utero have also been recorded because they were thought to soothe the baby, and, perhaps help him or her to sleep!!

Through these familiar sounds the baby has already begun to learn a culture but does this immediate culture within the home and do the cultural experiences outside the home always remain the same?

Reflection 4

Reflect on the question above:

- What changes could occur that will affect the micro-culture in the home?
- Differentiate between minor and major changes.
- What will the impact be on the members of the family?
- How will the members of the family adjust to the changes?
- What support is available within the local community?
- How might you help a baby or very young child who attends your setting, and their parents, through changes such as those you have identified?

The cultural changes that might occur within the home will be very closely linked to the members of the immediate family and extended family. The changes could be those that occur when one of the parents or close relatives works away from home; there will be changes whilst that person is away and again, when they return, there is a change in the family dynamics. Different members of the family, through necessity, will take on different roles within the house when another member is absent. However small these changes are, they still have an impact. A simple example is perhaps the 'school run' which is usually facilitated by the person who is away. Another significant adult may have to take on the responsibility for ensuring a child is taken to school. A change that will have more of an impact on the family culture is when a family decides to have changes made to their accommodation, such as an extension which will ultimately provide better facilities for the family. However, the actual building process is very stressful. This kind of situation can completely change the family dynamics and culture within the home. The effect on a child's emotions can be huge, they may feel worried, frightened and overwhelmed.

One other very significant change for a child within the home culture is the Mother's return to work after maternity leave. Child care might have been arranged within the home with relatives or the employment of a nanny, possibly less of a change than attending an Early Years setting? However, as you are well aware, there is the opportunity for child care in a home environment through a childminder. Early Years settings such as nurseries or day care will also have been considered. The decision taken by the parent/parents or carer is usually related to the setting that they think would best suit their needs and, most importantly, the needs of their baby or young child.

These are some, very familiar, examples of changes that may occur within an immediate environment, but which lead to consideration of the different environments that a baby or child may then be exposed to. Bronfenbrenner (1979) cited by MacDougall and Brown (2016) named the concept of different environments, *ecological systems theory*. He divided the life experiences of children into two systems, the close home environment and people he named the *microsystem* and the wider experiences of two or more groups such as nursery, school and the local community *mesosystems*. Beyond this are the political and economic influences, *exosystems*, and in their widest context, there are the globally influenced *macrosystems*.

How would you as a Key Person in your setting help and support a baby or young child and his or her parents or carers through a change being considered or experienced at home? How would you know these changes might be happening? Perhaps the information has not been shared with you? You will, if you have a good partnership with the parent or carer and you know the baby or young child really well, perhaps notice changes in the baby's or young child's behaviour. Perhaps, having been quite happy to separate from their Mother or carer, he or she has shown that they are finding it hard to separate, he or she has separation anxiety.

Reflection 5

Consider the environment within your setting and refer back to Reflection 2:

■ What type of culture do you have in the setting?

■ Are you able to use Bronfenbrenner's ecological systems theory?

■ Do you think you have what have been referred to earlier as microcultures within your setting?

■ Do you consider this inevitable?

■ How would you manage these different microcultures?

Early Years settings vary greatly, as you all appreciate. Even across a group of nurseries under the same ownership and management, different cultures will exist and within each setting, each room will have a different culture. First, you should consider the different types of childcare. Which type will a parent or carer choose.? How will the culture experienced during visits and their first attendances influence their choice?

You have already begun to consider the cultures in your settings.

Reflection 6

Is there a culture of respect, and who should be respected?

Is there a culture of inclusion and equality of opportunity?

How are these cultures managed and maintained?

What changes would you make to ensure that the culture is respectful to all and that there is inclusion and equality of opportunity?

How has modern technology affected the culture in your setting?

Is there a culture of leadership and change which involves and values all members of staff?

Following on from these cultures, which form a sound basis for a welcoming, respectful, inclusive culture, other cultures that should be present within Early Years settings include:

■ a culture within each room of reflection and reflective practice, collaboration and cooperation, values and ideals

- a culture of calmness and learning through play, exploration and acquisition of knowledge appropriate to the developmental age and stage of the babies and young children

- a culture of support for the acquisition of a second language

- a culture of risk and challenge.

Reading and checking through the list above it can be seen that the notion of culture can be related to every aspect of provision within each Early Years setting.

The focus is now related to the language experiences and needs of children for whom English is a second language. The emotional needs for these children is recognised in relation to their cultural needs experienced at home.

> Advances in infant psychology give scientific foundation to a theory of human motivation for learning cultural rituals and conventions, including language. Children are 'story seeking' from the start, wanting to learn a new way of expressing and sharing experience. Each child's Self actively grows by sharing meaning in relationships, in the family and in a familiar community.
>
> (Trevarthen 2011 pp. 174–175)

This full quote from Trevarthen is appropriate at this point but each sentence has been used separately to support ideas or provoke thought about your provision and the way you work in a multicultural environment to recognise and support each culture and language. You will read them after case study one.

Support provided in Early Years settings for acquisition of a second language

Exposure to a different language could be considered to be one of the most significant cultural differences that a child or adult may experience. There are many Early Years settings working with children and parents from many different cultures, that is, they are multi-cultural. It has been identified that *diversity and bi-lingualism are increasingly becoming the norm.* Roberts (2010). Consequently, there will be many children for whom English is the second language. Many of those children were perhaps born in the United Kingdom and therefore, it may be assumed that they have been exposed to both their mother tongue and to English. However, this might not always be so because there may be members of immigrant families who have not learned to speak English. There may also be children who have only just arrived in the United Kingdom and have no knowledge of the English language. Many settings do have members of staff who speak a child's first language who will be able to communicate with the child and their parents. However, this cannot be taken for granted because many countries, such as India, have many, many different dialects and regional accents.

In these situations, every effort will be made by staff to help families settle into the Early Years setting. An interpreter will, or should be, invited to attend the setting when the family first arrives and then, as necessary. Staff will ask the parents or carers to teach essential words in their mother tongue to the Key Person. Also, the Picture Exchange Communication System (PECS) may be used with very young children. This, as you know, enables a child to point to a picture to indicate what they would like to play with or perhaps to eat. It has been recorded that children who are learning two languages may have some delay in acquiring language skills, Bligh et al. (2013). However, recent research and a personal example challenge the original theories of language delay.

> Raising children bilingually is sometimes believed to cause language delay,
> though evidence does not support this position. Raising children bilingually
> neither increases nor reduces the chance of language disorder or delay.
>
> (Baker, 2000 p. 127)

Consider the following provocations.

Provocation 2a

A family where the Mother is Spanish, and the father is English have a young child of four years-of-age who is here known as Juan. The Mother speaks Spanish to Juan most of the time whilst the father speaks Spanish at home but English within other contexts. The English grandparents speak in English. By the time Juan was two and a half years of age he was able to speak both languages fluently with no Spanish accent when speaking English and no English accent when speaking Spanish. It was amazing to listen to Juan swapping from one language to the other. He was understanding all that was said to him, including the cultural nuances as he was being joked with and teased. He answered correctly in both languages. He had been exposed to both languages and cultures from the day he was born.

In contrast and outside of the family home, in school:

Provocation 2b

A little boy of six years of age moved to Spain with his family. He will here be known as Harry. Harry spoke no Spanish. He started school there and was taken to school by his parents on the first day and collected by them at the end of the day when he was asked by them how his day had been. Fine he said but they keep calling me, 'asientese'. Asientese means sit down. Oh dear, one wonders how his first day really progressed. In some respects, this provocation is funny but in others sad for that child. The meaning of the word was explained to him so that he did sit down when required to do so on the succeeding days. Not understanding the language or the local culture within the area and within school must have been very difficult for a while, especially emotionally. However, he did settle and learned to speak Spanish fluently. There were no reports of him exhibiting a silent period.

Bligh (2013) presented an interesting case study about a four-year-old Japanese child who attended a Reception Class, having attended a day nursery for two years before starting school. She had not spoken at all in either setting. There were concerns that this might be due to selective mutism which was the diagnosis given by a speech and language therapist. Bligh was not convinced because it is documented that there is a period when a child is learning a second language known as the silent period. It is a time when a child who is being exposed to a second language is participating but silently. Home visits were made, the child was heard speaking in the mother tongue and in English. Techniques were implemented to help the child communicate where there was no pressure to speak in front of the whole class. Gradually, speech developed (Bligh 2013 pp. 18–32).

This is a very short outline of the case study and research presented by Bligh. See further reading for the full case study and research. It is referred to here because a similar but not so long-lasting scenario was experienced by a younger child from the Japanese Culture.

Case study 1

This is a similar case study to that presented by Bligh. A two-year-old Japanese child, to be known as Kiki, moved into the area and attended the local Day Care Unit five days a week. The Mother had a good level of spoken and written English, but Kiki only spoke her mother tongue. Prior to Kiki starting at the setting cultural artefacts were purchased for the home corner and a few children's books in Japanese were purchased. A few Japanese words were learned by the Key Person. At first this was a very emotional experience for Kiki and for the Key Person. She was demonstrating very obvious separation anxiety. The Mother worked nearby and was able to visit during her lunch time. Gradually with continuity of care and sensitive, gentle responses to Kiki, she began to settle. She started to play with the familiar resources in the home corner and she began to play with and communicate with the other children. Her development of English language was slow but, very gently, staff would point to items such as the toys and the foods she was offered, stating the name of each item in English. Kiki gradually started using the English words which she had been taught. In fact, her acquisition of her second language was rapid. However, her Mother reported several months later that Kiki spoke good English, but would not speak to her Mother in Japanese. She did understand Japanese when spoken to and would speak to her Father, who was still in Japan, on the telephone.

Although Kiki did not demonstrate silent participation in the way Bligh reported she did present with a reluctance to speak in her first language. In some ways the silent period can be paralleled with selective mutism, but Bligh cited (Clarke, 1997 and Tabors, 1997) who see the silent period *as a normal stage in additional language acquisition.* It was also thought that the experience of being exposed to a completely different culture within the setting for many hours each week could impact and extend the silent period. This might also relate to the absence of the family culture and the fact that the first language appears to have been disregarded by the setting. One of the findings from Bligh's research was:

> The silent period presents as a phase of intense learning, through fractionally increasing participation.
>
> (Bligh 2013 p. 25)

Silent participation has been researched by Kato, cited in Bligh 2013, who compared the *learning of Japanese students* with the learning of indigenous American students. Kato found that Japanese students *saw silence as a legitimate form of classroom participation.* The students thought that *note-taking, listening and reading assigned books were alternative participation.*

Bligh returns to the experiences of bilingual young children in Early Years settings, voicing the opinion that these children are already disadvantaged by experiencing cultural discontinuity between home and school.

> Each child's Self actively grows by sharing meaning in relationships, in the family and in a familiar community'
>
> (Trevarthen 2011 pp. 174–175)

We must ensure, within our settings, that each person's culture is taken into consideration; their language should be acknowledged, as should the different culture within their home setting. The Key Person in the Early Years setting should consider inviting the parents/carers in to show the other children pictures of their home and perhaps their traditional costumes. Photographs of a child's home that can be kept in the Early Years setting and can be shared with the Key Person and the other children would help to ensure the child's culture is being acknowledged. When the child has the language skills in the second language, he or she could be encouraged to create their own story to share with the group.

> Children are 'story seeking' from the start, wanting to learn new way of expressing and sharing experience.
>
> (Trevarthen 2011 pp. 174–175)

Vivian Gussin Paley has written several books about the use of story-telling with young children, aged from two to four years of age. She found that encouraging children to tell stories improved their listening skills, memory recall, language skills and behavioural issues. Two of her books are listed as recommendations for further reading; they are easy to read but very informative and provide food for thought about our own practice.

For children attending Early Years settings without knowledge of the language of the setting this is obviously a very emotional time. Their emotional needs are very strong; it must be very stressful. It is very hard not being able to make yourself understood or not understanding what is being said to you. Language must be the hardest part of a new culture to learn. It must be very frightening because it is so strange to them. However, if the Key Person is gentle, shows understanding and allows the child to explore the new surroundings if they show a desire to do so, the child should gradually settle. It is important for Key Persons to learn about the cultural norms and the expectations of the parents or carers. Some key words in their mother tongue, even greetings, should help. As Whinnett states when considering Froebel's Principles

> Each child's identity is formed in relation to self, family and community. Everyone working with young children has to learn as much as possible from parents to understand the child.
>
> (Whinnett 2012 p. 135)

Examples of cultural norms and expectations

Cultural norms and expectations vary across each country and across the world. Pinker provided a wonderful insight into the culture of the Kung San tribe in the

Kalahari Desert, South Africa. Apparently, they believed that children should be taught to sit, stand and walk. To this end they:

> Carefully pile sand around their infants to prop them upright with the result that, every one of these infants soon sits up on its own.
>
> (Pinker 1995 p. 40)

This approach to physical development is completely alien to our culture where babies are allowed to learn to sit, stand and walk, when they are ready. However, he moves on to give examples of cultures who do not use Motherese; they think it is unnecessary to encourage children to speak by speaking to them because they do not understand what you say!! I would challenge that statement because language acquisition and understanding are not just linked to the ability to speak. They are linked to body language, facial expression and often to routines. I firmly believe that babies and young children do begin to learn their mother tongue before they actually speak, through the constant repetition of vocabulary used during proto-conversations, singing lullabies and nursery rhymes. They also learn from the cues of routines, for example, when babies see bibs being given to them, they start to cry and appear desperate to have their feeds. They show a development of understanding about key cues linked to routines and anticipate what is coming next.

Provocation 3

When working in a children's home where children used to stay for short periods of time, I always used to encourage parents or carers to explain to very young children that they were going to stay in the home. The age of the child was irrelevant because I believed that older children would understand but that babies would recognise the length of the phrases used by the parents or carers and would recognise the similar phrases used by the Key Persons. This can, perhaps, be considered in relation to the work by Trevarthen who identified the musicality and metre observed in proto-conversations.

Consider the provocation above, could this be so, and have you had similar experiences to reflect on and analyse?

Singing and nursery rhymes are closely linked to continuing the generational culture and the culture within baby's and young children's homes as well as the development of language and literacy skills. Bruce and Spratt (2011) provide strong evidence of the importance of music, singing and movement in the development of language, literacy and communication abilities. Many of the songs for older children, that have been included in their book, are also described as multicultural, in that they are appropriate for all cultures. Examples of these multicultural songs are action songs such as,

1. There was a princess long, long ago;

2. Here we go round the mulberry bush;

3. Three little monkeys jumping on the bed.

Early Years settings all include time for singing and, from experience, sing more often than once a day. Singing can be calming, exciting and emotional, and can provide opportunities for movement and dancing all so important for the development of language and literacy and the development of self-awareness.

> Their bodies need moving, and their minds need discovering – of what is real, imagined and remembered. They want, not 'stimulation', but lively company that loves them and respects their eagerness to learn.
>
> (Trevarthen 2009 p. 1)

> Research on songs for infants in many languages has taught us how we share story-telling underneath, or beyond, the spoken word – in the body
>
> (Ekerdal and Merker 2009, cited by Trevarthen 2009 p. 5)

The culture of technology

The impact of the increasingly rapid development of technology was introduced at the beginning of the chapter; it will now be considered in more detail. Modern technology has undoubtedly had an impact on most of the world, especially since the invention and introduction of televisions, mobile telephones, computers, laptops, play-stations and tablets. The speed with which technology has evolved is extremely fast, in fact almost as soon as a new computer has been purchased, the technology has progressed and the systems within the computer are 'out of date.' Palmer cites McLuhan, 'a Canadian media visionary who named this phenomenon 'electric speed.' (Palmer 2006 p. 13)

What has been the impact of 'electric speed' on our culture? It has been profound; the culture and lifestyles of today cannot really be compared with the culture and lifestyles of 50 years ago. Lives are so busy. This is partly due to the fact that Mothers have been encouraged to return to work and children, therefore, attend Early Years settings or are cared for by extended family, often grandparents. Everyone is bombarded with advertisements on television, bill boards, throughout underground stations as one is travelling on the escalators, via email and 'snail mail.' There are also pressures to fill every part of the day with activities, such as attending the gym, running, football, tennis, yoga, baby massage, baby yoga, beavers, cubs, brownies, scouts . . . the list is long. The examples of activities given here are important because they are encouraging physical fitness and development and participation within local communities, BUT the point being made here is that in trying to participate in activities before and after work takes time when lives are already so busy. When is time spent with the family, especially with the children? The challenges and pressures faced by parents and carers today are many. When is there time to prepare and cook well-balanced, nutritious meals and sit together, round a table to eat and to chat? Where do many children and adults sit to eat their meals? The culture of today is frenetic but can also encourage isolation.

Isolation of family members, especially as children grow older, occurs when they have computers and televisions in their own bedrooms. However, this isolation can also occur within the home in family rooms because, often, adults and children are all using their own mobile phones, laptops and tablets to access games or social media and to watch a different programme than the one on the television. There is no conversation or interest in the other members of the family who are present. Very young babies can be placed in front of a television, children of two to ten years of age may be using a tablet. They become mesmerised by the rapid movements on the screen in front of them. There is absolutely no interaction between adults and children. There is no imagination being used. When the tablet or television is turned off the children are upset, they do not know what to do with themselves, they are unable to play, they just flop around.

The appeal of tablets with games for very young children could be linked to Piaget's sensory motor phase of learning and development, with a swipe or tap of the screen with that pointed index finger which babies of the age of approximately one year love to use, and to Piaget's theory of 'cause and effect.' There is an immediate change in the picture on the screen, BUT what do they learn from the change on the screen?

The effects of isolation and the zombie inducing effect of continuously using a laptop are possibly part of the reason for a rise in problems with the mental health of children today. The immediate change of mood and enjoyment in play is now considered.

The culture of learning, play, exploration and outdoors play

Children have lively spirits that want affectionate care, joy in play, things and places to explore, a chance to dream, sing and dance about, and difficult tasks that test their will to move and feel.

(Trevarthen 2009 p. 1)

A walk with family members, is stimulating and enjoyable, provided the adults do not spend their time on their mobile phones. The adults should be interacting with their children, running and jumping, discussing the surroundings, looking for birds and insects, identifying the trees and flowers, watching trains go under bridges, discussing the cars driving by, helping the children with road safety, climbing trees, building dens or going to a play park where they can climb, swing and invent games. The list of opportunities is endless. During these activities children will use their imagination and will 'come alive.' They quickly change from being mesmerised zombies into energised, enthusiastic, involved, active learners. They will take risks, if allowed to. Generally, adults have, sadly, become very risk averse, wrapping their children in cotton-wool. They do not like them getting dirty – what a shame; what is more fun than digging and playing in the mud and making dens out of natural resources? The children are exploring, finding out about nature and the world they live in and, as they get older, they share, make rules and support one another in their play. They are creating their own cultures of learning. Yes, adults should be there to help, to provide, in Froebel's words, *'freedom with guidance.'* But the play should be led by the children.

> Culture is activity of thought, and the receptiveness to beauty and human feeling. Scraps of information have nothing to do with it.
>
> (Whitehead 1929 p. 1, cited in Trevarthen 2009 p. 1)

The learning experiences in the last paragraph should also be achievable in Early Years settings. This is not always easy, as you know, because of building types and the locations of settings. The EYFS recommends that children should have free access to indoor and outdoor play at all times, if possible. Settings where there is no immediate access to outdoor play are encouraged to take the children out for walks each day.

If children do not exercise regularly, as is encouraged when children are allowed to sit at play stations, or watch television, or play games on a tablet or mobile phone, there are other implications for the development of health problems. For example, at the same time as watching television, they may be snacking on foods such as crisps, sweets, very sweet cup-cakes, chocolate bars and fatty foods, not eating a well-balanced, healthy meal. This has resulted in a very high percentage of children and adults being obese. Here are some of the published statistics giving the percentages of obese children from Public Health England 2015:

- more than 1 in 5 children are overweight or obese when they begin school

- almost 1 in 3 children are overweight or obese by the time they leave primary school

- obesity rates are highest in the most deprived 10% of the population – approximately twice that of the least deprived 10%

■ obesity rates are higher in some ethnic minority groups of children (particularly Black African and Bangladeshi ethnicities) and for children with disability, especially those with learning difficulties.

(Public Health England 2015 – Facts about obesity)

Obesity is a worrying trend that can lead to conditions such as asthma, diabetes, hypertension, cancer, heart disease, or stroke and is linked to cultural changes such as eating fast foods, neither eating home prepared foods nor eating as a family and eating more foods like those listed above.

Returning to the theme of healthy exercise, consider the questions in Reflection 7.

Reflection 7

Reflect on the outdoor experiences provided in your Early Years setting:

■ If you have an outdoor play area or garden – how is it used?

■ Do the children play outside for most of the time?

■ If you do not have an outdoor area – when do the children play outside?

■ How would you change the outdoor area and access to it?

■ Do all members of staff participate in outdoor play?

■ What resources would you expect to see in the area?

■ How would you include resources that reflect the cultures of the children attending your setting?

Whilst it is imperative that children play outside, we cannot ignore the technological culture of the world. It has its place; when used for administration in Early Years settings, electronic devices are invaluable, although when first introduced they were used with caution and some suspicion. Computers, mobile phones and the internet have revolutionised the way that we communicate. It is so fast; we do not have to wait weeks for a reply to a communication – well not usually. However, it has had a profound effect on our children. Richard House, the editor of Too Much, Too Soon, is Steiner trained. He and his colleagues were and still are very concerned about the effects of technology on very young children. Steiner nurseries do not permit any form of technology inside the childcare and educational areas as mentioned in Chapter 3.

A point for discussion and debate – do you consider this is right in the climate of our current culture? One could say technology rules our lives, and so . . .? Should children be exposed to technology to a degree? This could also form a debate to share with parents to seek their views? It may also be a question parents ask you.

Modern technology and parents returning to work have been shown to have an impact on our culture. They have also affected the way that children are parented, and how they behave. Morris (2015) discusses the three main styles of parenting authoritarian, permissive or authoritative, highlighting that the main style today is authoritative, where parents see their role as providing support and guidance, rather than telling a child what to do or allowing a child to be a 'free spirit.' The changes in the styles of parenting are very much linked to Mothers returning to work, wanting to spend quality time with their children and not wanting to be saying, don't do this and don't do that. These sentiments are possibly linked to a sense of guilt. However, children do require guidance, they need to be taught right from wrong and to be taught about consequences. There should be boundaries set in place for unwanted behaviours, but parents should be firm, fair and kind. It is not easy being a parent!! It is not easy being an Early Years Practitioner and Key Person.

Conclusion

The response of the adult to the emotional needs of children remains virtually unchanged.

> Their bodies need moving, and their minds need discovering – of what is real, imagined and remembered. They want, not 'stimulation', but lively company that loves them and respects their eagerness to learn. Everything they know and do can be shared with affectionate partners. They cannot grow well, make friends or learn if they are tired, hungry, frightened, angry, bored or ashamed. These are constitutional givens of human beings from which all needs and social rights arise.
>
> (Trevarthen 2009 p. 1)

However, in the United Kingdom, because of the constraints placed upon Early Years Practitioners by Government and all the related advice, culture is changing all the time – as it is worldwide. An example of government pressure is the Early Years Foundation Stage Framework that was introduced for implementation in all settings from September 2008. It was a very full document with supporting DVDs and information to enable Early Years Practitioners to respond to the needs of children and to extend their knowledge. The Framework included the Birth to Three Framework which had been well received and implemented by the Early Years workforce. The experiences of the children improved, the focus on play was welcomed, resulting in the improvement of play experiences in many of the settings. However, the impact of continuing pressure from government has resulted in a gradual 'dumbing down' of the framework. The result is a very slim, changed document that has gradually decreased in size from 2012 to 2014, 2016 and 2017. The point about a curriculum reflecting the requirements of the Government was discussed by Nuttall (2003) in relation to changes in the New Zealand curriculum, Te Whariki. When first introduced the curriculum was seen to be vulnerable because

> curriculum development is fundamentally a political act.
>
> (Nuttall 2003 p. 11)

A further point that is so pertinent to Early Years in the United Kingdom and related to this chapter is that

> early childhood education is a distinctive cultural form in its own right.
>
> (Nuttall 2003 p. 11)

How very true. You as Early Years Practitioners and Key Persons should remember this quote so that, when challenged about your practices relating to the emotional needs of children, you are able to articulate the reasons for your practice. You will be able to speak about the fact that their play and learning are child led. That you are offering play experiences that provide freedom for the children to choose and lead their play with an adult nearby to guide them. You will also be able to explain your ethos for working with parents and carers to ensure that each child's native language and culture are met. You are meeting their individual and emotional needs following communication with parents and carers and your observations recorded in your setting.

Further reading

Bruner, J. (1997) *The Culture of Education*, USA: Harvard Press
Bruner provides historic and current perspectives of education. It will extend your knowledge of theories of education which have only been mentioned in this chapter.

Byron, T (2008) *The Byron Review* http://webarchive.nationalarchives.gov.uk/2010040810 5219/http://www.dcsf.gov.uk/byronreview/ accessed 12 December 2017.
This review focuses mainly on the dangers of children using the internet when unsupervised. It will help you when working with parents to provide substantive evidence from research.

Ferre Leavers Emotional Well-being and Involvement Scales, cited by Katherine Lewis, on line 2011– https://www.earlylearninghq.org.uk/blog/page/34/ accessed 12 December 2017.
These involvement and well-being scales provide information to help you analyse observations of the children in your settings.

Paley, V G (1999) *The Kindness of Children*, London: Harvard University Press Vivian Gussin Paley visits a London Nursery School where she uses observation and interaction, including recording, in order to bring out the children's stories with them. She sees amazing, almost humbling acts of kindness and acceptance of children's needs by the children, through story-telling, that an adult may find it difficult to understand and respond to.

Paley, V G (2001) *Mrs Tully's Room, A Childcare Portrait*, London: Harvard University Press Vivian Gussin Paley visits Mrs Tully's Room in a nursery in Chicago, Illinois, USA where she observes Mrs Tully working with two year-olds, sharing their stories. It provides strong evidence of the value of encouraging children to tell their own stories at this very young age.

Woodhead, (1998) The Cultural Worlds of Early Childhood, London: Routledge
The title of this book explains the content.

References

Baker, C (2000) *The Care and Education of Young Bilinguals: An Introduction for Professionals*, Clevedon: Short Run Press Ltd

Bligh, C; Chambers, S; Davison, C; Lloyd, I; Musgrave, J; O'Sullivan, J and Waltham, S. (2013) *Well-being in the Early Years* Norwich: Critical

Bruce, T and Spratt, J (2011) *Essentials of Literacy from 0 – 7 – A Whole child approach to communication, language and literacy*, 2nd Edition. London: Sage

Bruner, J (1997) *The Culture of Education*, USA: Harvard Press

Byron, T (2008) *The Byron Review* http://webarchive.nationalarchives.gov.uk/2010040810 5219/http://www.dcsf.gov.uk/byronreview/ accessed 12 December 2017

Clarke, P (1996) Investigating Second Language Acquisition in Preschools. PhD thesis, Latrobe University. Published in Clarke (2009), in Bligh et al (2013) *Well-being in the Early Years* Northwich: Critical Publishing

Cole, M (1998) Culture in Development in *Cultural Worlds of Early Childhood*, eds Faulkner, D; Littleton, K and Woodhead, M, London: Routledge

Elfer, P; Goldschmied, E and Selleck, D (2003) *Key Persons in the Nursery*, London: David Fulton

Georgeson, J and Payler, J eds (2013) *International Perspectives on Early Childhood Education and Care*, Berkshire: Open University Press

Haralambos, M and Holborn, M (2000) *Sociology, Themes and Perspectives*, 5th Edition, London: Collins

MacDougall, I and Brown, J (2016) The Foundation Years; Babies, in *The Early Years Handbook for Students and Practitioners*, Ed Trodd, L; Oxon: Routledge

Morris, K (2015) *Promoting Positive Behaviour in the Early Years*, Maidenhead: Open University Press

NHS (2016) *Mindfulness* www.nhs.uk accessed 1 March 2018

Nuttall, J (2003) *Weaving Te Whariki*, New Zealand: New Zealand Council for Educational Research

Paley, V G (1999) *The Kindness of Children*, London: Harvard University Press

Paley, V G (2001) *Mrs Tully's Room, A Childcare Portrait*, London: Harvard University Press

Palmer, S (2006) *Toxic Childhood*, London: Orion Books

Piaget, J (1950/2002) *The Psychology of Intelligence*, Reprint, London: Routledge Classics

Pinker, S (1995) *The Language Instinct, Penguin*: London: The Penguin Group

Public Health England (2015) *Guidance Childhood obesity: applying All Our Health*, Gov.UK

Reber, A S (1995) *The Penguin Dictionary of Psychology*, London: Penguin

Roberts, R (2010) *Self-Esteem and Early Learning*, London: Sage

Siraj-Blatchford, I (2010) Diversity, Inclusion and Learning in the Early Years in *Contemporary Issues in the Early Years;* 5th Edition, eds Duffy, B and Pugh, G; London: Sage

Standards and Testing Agency (2016) *Early Years Foundation Stage Profile Handbook* https://www.gov.uk/government/uploads/system/uploads/attachment_data/file/564249/2017_EYFSP_handbook_v1.1.pdf accessed 1 March 2018

Tabors, P (1997) One Child, Two Languages, in Bligh et al (2013) *Well-being in the Early Years* Northwich: Critical Publishing

The Concise Oxford Dictionary (1995); 9th Edition Ed. Thompson, D; Oxford: Oxford University Press

Thomas, E (2017) Exploring residential mobility: Learning about how young children experience the transition of moving-house and how adults can best support them, Presented at the TACTYC Conference, Birmingham, November 2017

Thomas, N (2001) Listening to Children. in *Children in Society*, eds Foley, P; Roche, J; Tucker, S, Hampshire: (Palgrave Macmillan) Open University Press

Trevarthen, C (1998) The Child's Need to Learn a Culture in *Cultural Worlds of Early Childhood*, eds Faulkner, D; Littleton, K and Woodhead, M; London: Routledge

Trevarthen, C (July 2004) *Making Friends with Infants*, Paper presented at Pen Green Conference: Northampton

Trevarthen, C (November 2005) Conference Presentation at Pen Green: Northampton.

Trevarthen, C (2009) Why Attachment Matters in Sharing Meaning – HUMAN NEEDS & HUMAN SENSE: THE NATURAL SCIENCE OF MEANING, Paper presented on Friday 11 September 2009 Glasgow Marriott Hotel, 500 Argyle Street, Glasgow file:///G:/Book%20-%20Emotional%20Needs/Colwyn-Trevarthen-2009-Human-Needs-and-Human-Sense.pdf accessed 12 December 2017

Trevarthen, C (2011) What young children give to their learning, making education work to sustain a community and its culture, in '*European Early Childhood Education Research Journal, The Journal of the European Early Childhood Education Research Association*, pp. 173–193 Oxon: Routledge, Taylor Francis Group

Whinnett, J (2012) Gifts and Occupations: Froebel's Gifts (Wooden Block Play) and Occupations (Construction and Workshop Experiences) Today, in *Early Childhood Practice – Froebel Today*, Ed. Tina Bruce London: Sage

Woodhead, M (1998) The Cultural Worlds of Early Childhood, London: Routledge

Websites

https://www.heritagedaily.com/2013/10/roman-skulls-discovered-under-liverpool-street-station/99123 accessed 23 November 2017

http://www.multilingualliving.com/2010/05/31/does-bilingualism-multilingualism-cause-language-delay/ accessed 11 December 2017

6 Conclusion

> ## Key themes included in this book are:
>
> - The **emotional needs** of babies and very young children and how to respond appropriately to their needs
>
> - Brain development from conception through to adolescence and beyond
>
> - The importance of secure attachment, separation anxiety and the effects of insecure attachment
>
> - Reflections on the importance of in-depth observation to ensure effective response to the **emotional needs** of young children
>
> - The important role Early Years Practitioners have in the lives of the children in their care, particularly the Key Person Role, working in partnership with parents and their position in a multi-professional team
>
> - The impact of different cultures experienced by very young children, such as home and childcare settings
>
> - Reflections on the effects of the adult's own childhood experiences when responding to young children
>
> - Considerations and reflections on the environment and quality of care provided in your settings
>
> - Provision of a calm, caring environment that responds to the emotional and individual learning needs of every child in their setting.

The intention of this book has been to focus your thoughts on the **emotional needs** of babies and very young children, rather than emotional development. This conclusion provides a precis of some of the findings and discussions from each chapter, as well as repeating the main themes identified in the conclusion to each chapter. It brings together and highlights the interconnectedness of the main topics discussed and explained in the book. It is imperative that all persons, Early Years Practitioners, paediatric nurses, teachers, social workers, health visitors and paediatricians, paediatric psychologists and paediatric psychotherapists understand and are enabled to respond to the emotional needs of babies and very young children.

It is imperative that the theme of emotional needs is maintained because there is not a single experience in life when emotions are not influencing needs and behaviours. However, positive experiences during the early years, of secure attachment to a Mother and / or other significant adult who responds to a baby's or young child's emotional needs, will enable his or her progression and development throughout his or her life. Whereas an insecure attachment results in stress which may affect the development of the brain and the formation of neural pathways, as discussed in Chapters 1 and 2.

Baby's and very young children's emotional needs have remained the focus throughout each chapter. There is such strong evidence from Bowlby and the Robertsons, and the findings of neuroscientific research linking attachment theory to the development of the brain. This research resulted in changes in policy for visiting hours in children's wards in the 1960s, gradually increasing from 30 minutes each day, or in some instances no visiting, to free visiting, as discussed in the Introduction. During the 1990s, the demographics of childcare and education began to change. Women were being encouraged to return to work, with the result that there was a rapid expansion in the number of young children attending day care settings. It was the beginning of a Key Person or Worker being allocated for each child attending an Early Years setting. This was initially seen as good practice, as identified by Goldschmied and Jackson (1994/2004) and Elfer, Goldschmied and Selleck (2003). However, as detailed in Chapter 3 the Key Person approach became mandatory when the Early Years Foundation Stage (EYFS) (DCSF 2008) was implemented and each child had to be allocated a Key Person. The Key Person approach (Elfer et al. 2003) has not always been implemented with ease, as Elfer et al. and also Goouch and Powell (2013) found in their research into practices the 'The Baby Room.'

To ensure they respond to their key children and meet their needs, Key Persons have been encouraged to work in partnership with parents in all Early Years settings, since the implementation of the EYFS (2008). Forming a partnership with parents has evolved from being the role of the manager to that of the Key Person with the support of the manager. In Chapter 3 the role of the Key Person was covered, as was the importance of working with parents in Chapter 4 and the importance of respecting the different cultures of each family, community and Early Years setting in Chapter 5; these are interwoven and interdependent aspects of the Key Person's role and are essential for responding fully to children's emotional needs. The findings of research, especially in relation to attachment theory and the development of the brain have had an impact on practice, as discussed in each chapter.

Chapter 1: Development of the brain in relation to the emotional needs of very young children

Neuroscience has been considered firstly through the structure, function and development of the brain from conception, through the first 1001 days of life. This includes references to the changes in the neural connections and neural pathways during adolescence and during adulthood. The brain forms and reforms significant neural connections and creates new neural pathways; this is described as 'plasticity' and is present throughout life. Formation of neural connections and pathways is very rapid in the first two to three years of life and is dependent, partly but very importantly, on the sensitive, gentle, reassuring and respectful responses of significant adults to the emotional needs of a baby or very young child. It is dependent on the formation of secure attachments to a significant adult, usually the Mother or a Mother figure/carer.

Shore (1997) spoke about nature and nurture but also included the effects of the environment on the development of the brain:

> Human development hinges on the interplay between nature and nurture.
>
> It was assumed that the genes we are born with determine how our brains develop. Neuroscientists have found that throughout the entire process of development, beginning even before birth, the brain is affected by environmental conditions, including the kind of nourishment, care, surroundings, and stimulation an individual receives. The impact of the environment is dramatic and specific, not merely influencing the general direction of development, but actually affecting how the intricate circuitry of the brain is wired.
>
> (Shore, R 1997 p. ix)

Advances in neuroscience have been acknowledged in relation to the speed of brain development during a child's first three years of life. However, it remains very important when working with babies and very young children to heed warnings about using the 'sensitive developmental periods' to ensure the children learn as much as possible during these periods, especially the period from birth to three years. Remember that *'learning opportunities need to be available to all ages'* (Blakemore and Frith 2005 p. 35). It is essential to respond to the individual needs of each child to ensure they receive the care and education that is appropriate at that time. It is of immense importance to use observations to identify what a child is able to do, not what he or she cannot do, in order to ensure that a child's brain continues to develop well, that each child has a sense of well-being and her or his emotional needs are being met. It remains imperative that you use your observations to identify their interests and respond to the learning and developmental needs of each child.

Shore, in the quote above, spoke of the brain being affected by 'the kind of environmental conditions . . . and stimulation.' Keep in mind that this says, 'the kind of . . . stimulation.' Overstimulation can have adverse effects. Remember, any baby or young child who is overstimulated or expected to participate in play or activities that do not reflect their individual needs and interests may become disinterested and overwhelmed because the activities do not support their emotional and learning needs. This is often referred to as being 'hot-housed.' Gopnick, Meltzoff and Kuhl 2001), Moss 2014 and House 2011 raised concerns about the impact this was having on provision and as House said, 'expecting too much too soon', from very young children.

The availability of technology such as MRI scanners has resulted in discoveries in neuroscience since the 1990s that have linked attachment theory to the development of the brain (Carter 2010 and Blakemore and Frith 2005). The findings confirm that insecure attachment has a profound effect on the development of the brain. Fewer neural connections are made with the result that the brain has been found to be smaller in children with insecure attachment, compared to the brain size in a child with a secure attachment, due to the larger number of neural connections present (see the images that have been included in Chapter 1). It is not only secure and insecure attachments that affect the development of the brain. Regression and developmental delay in language, cognition and physical skills may be the result of injury, viral or bacterial infections. Or a congenital condition may also affect the number of neural connections formed.

Therefore, should there be concerns about a baby or child attending your settings, it is important not to 'jump to conclusions' or to assume there isn't really a problem, it is just, 'one of those things' or 'a bad day.' Good communication with parents or carers is essential and well recorded, detailed observations must be taken regularly and analysed. The analysis should be shared with other members of the staff team, the parents or carers and other professionals, to ensure your continued responses to each child's needs.

Chapter 2: Attachment theory

The importance of secure attachment and the results of insecure attachment explored in this chapter cannot be overemphasised. John Bowlby has been cited by many, such as Freud, Trevarthen, Holmes and Barlow, as the person who initially influenced our practice today. He identified the need for each child to be given the opportunity to form a secure attachment with their first carer. The first carer should have the ability to demonstrate a sensitive responsiveness Barlow and Svanberg (2010) and be attuned to the infant's needs (Holmes 2001). Bowlby's theory was questioned by some researchers prior to research by neuroscientists during the 1990s. The results obtained using technology to scan the brain substantiated the need for each baby and young child to form a secure attachment with a significant adult, the Mother or first carer. The main point that has been woven throughout the chapter is the importance of the adult's responses to the emotional needs of a baby or young child to enable progression and development throughout his or her life.

There is encouragement to reflect on your own practice by reading case studies, accessing the films recorded by the Robertsons and using the related reflections. Using these case studies and reflections should enable you to implement changes that may improve the responses of Practitioners to the emotional needs of the children in your care. The importance of the Key Person has been reaffirmed and the resultant effects on each key child considered. Further reading has been recommended to expand and deepen your knowledge about attachment theory still further. Your role as a Key Person has also been referenced in relation to the requirements of the EYFS and Government policy. The requirements of the EYFS and Government policy will always fuel debate but your role as a Key Person is vital in relation to the emotional needs of very young children. As discussed throughout this chapter the formation of secure attachments and the effects of insecure attachments continue to be of paramount importance. This theme is explored in detail in Chapter three where the impact of attachment on the Key Person and implications for practice are considered in more detail.

Trevarthen believes:

> that the intensely shared pleasure of pride in knowledge and the skill that others applaud, as well as the feeling of shame in failure that threatens loss of relationship and hopeless isolation, are as important to the mental health of every human being as the emotions that seek comfort and care for the body. Indeed, I would suggest that attachment itself, if it is a friendship and not just the very asymmetric relationship between a weak and immature 'patient' and sensitive caregiver, is animated by emotions of shared discovery and the creation of inventive art.
>
> (Trevarthen 2004 p. 9)

Chapter 3: Key Persons: adults' responses to children

The role of the Early Years Practitioner, especially the role of the Key Person, in respect to every child's emotional needs has been identified as being very important. Remember and reflect on the fact that 'every child is unique' (EYFS 2017) and should, as Elfer et al. state, be:

experiencing a close relationship that is affectionate and reliable

(Elfer et al. (2003 p. 18)

To reinforce the role of the Key Person, you are there to:

- Welcome key children and their parents/carers

- Create a warm welcoming environment where each child's interests are provided for and reflected in the resources that are readily available and sit at the child's level

- Respond readily to the needs of each key child, maintain eye contact, mimic sounds of younger babies, repeat phrases and statements from older children to show you have heard and understood

- Listen to the children and their parents/carers

- Build strong, close (Manning-Morton, Thorpe 2006), reciprocal, trusting, knowledgeable relationships with the key children and their families

- Understand the different cultural approaches to parenting and the parents'/carers' expectations of the Early Years Setting

- Complete, record and analyse regular observations of key children

- Include the observations in the child's personal documentation

- Share information with other professionals who may be involved in the care and education of the child

- Provide information to parents/carers regarding extra support that may be required by the family

- Share with the child their successes and progression

- Share with and support the child when he/she is upset because they have experienced a sense of failure in their voyage of discovery, their play

- Work closely with parents to resolve situations when a child may require extra support

- Plan and provide for the care routines for key children having discussed these with the parents/carers. Does the child have a comforter, like to be cuddled to sleep, like food chopped, mashed or pureed etc. etc. Maintain the home routine for eating and sleeping whilst at the Early Years Setting

- Plan and provide play experiences based on the knowledge gained from parents and observations of key children's individual interests and learning needs.

The Role of the Key Person is very important for the baby or very young child.

Although the Key Person Approach was not in place when Piaget was alive he stated that:

> The human being is immersed right from birth in a social environment which affects him just as much as his physical environment. Society, even more, in a sense, than the physical environment, changes the very structure of the individual . . . Every relation between individuals (from two onwards) literally modifies them.
>
> (Piaget, 1950, reprinted 2002, pp. 171–172)

Goldschmied and Jackson provide the following thought about special relationships:

> Most of us have, or would like to have, a special relationship with some person on whom we can rely, a relationship that is significant and precious to us. If we are parted from that person we have ways of preserving continuity even through long separations . . .
>
> (Goldschmied and Jackson 2004 p. 42)

A way for a baby or young child to preserve continuity, even through separations longer than one day in an Early Years setting, is with what Winnicott described as a transitional object.

There has been some conflict in the role of the Key Person due to difficulties for both the Key Person and parent or carer about provision within the setting and also the closeness of relationships between the baby or young child and the Key Person. Elfer et al. also speak about nursery, day care and preschool experiences as being different from home experiences, which they should be. However,

> they do need to fit together well.
>
> (Elfer et al. 2003 p. 21)

Chapter 3 focused on the importance of your role as a Key Person who is required to form a strong reciprocal relationship with each of your key children and their families. This is a relationship that has a lasting impact on the future development of each child, on the increasing development of the brain and formation of neural connections through secure attachments and experiences formed in the first three years of life and linked to their emotional need to feel safe and secure. Dowling (2010) states, *'Babies' brains thrive on companionship'* which is supported by Trevarthen (2002) who speaks about *'children having an eagerness to learn . . . with companions they trust.'*

Elfer proposed that the:

> Quality of fit between the needs of the babies and their families and the particular circumstances and resources of each staff member is a very complex and intricate interaction.
>
> (Elfer 2004, paper presented at Pen Green)

This complex interaction, if understood and supported by the management, through supervision, should result in staff being able to respond to emotional needs of the children in their key groups more easily, because their own needs have been responded to. Early Years settings where the Key Person Approach is in place and supervision has been provided for staff have been highlighted as 'having quality provision' Elfer (2004). This is because staff who are closely supported in their role will be assisted and enabled to form the vital responsive relationships with their key children.

Chapter 4: Working with parents

'Working in Partnership with Parents' has been covered in detail to ensure that the individual care and learning needs of the children who attend your settings are met. The content of the chapter has very close links to the role of the Key Worker. The priority has remained the emotional needs of the children because, as stated throughout this book, if a child does not feel safe, secure, valued and respected, i.e. their emotional needs are not met, he or she will not be able to learn to their full potential. The impact of the past experiences of parents on their ability and style of parenting have been considered. This is because the emotional needs of very young children are inherently linked to the emotions experienced by their parents, particularly the Mother. But do remember that these possible barriers can gradually be overcome if you, as the Key Person, form a reciprocal, sensitive, respectful partnership with parents where a sense of trust has been developed and maintained.

Consideration has also been given to the impact of external sources and references made to Government initiatives, papers and legislation that affect choices of childcare and educational settings. Reports such as State of the Nation 2014 which report on the impact of good parenting on children's successes throughout life and the detrimental effects of poverty, have been included. The importance of the home learning environment and the parent or main carer as the expert about their child has been covered. The importance of forming reciprocal, sensitive relationships with parents and or carers has been stressed throughout the chapter. Many of the Early Years pioneers, psychologists and theorists who, for hundreds of years, have recognised the importance of the early years, observation and working with the family and their communities have been referenced. Thus your knowledge and understanding of the needs of very young children has been deepened from both historic and present day perspectives. Along with your deepening knowledge of the emotional needs of babies and young children, they will also enable you to articulate the ethos of your Early Years setting with more confidence. The information provided also helps you to respond to the needs of the parents or carers and to form strong informed partnerships with them. All of the above points endorse the very important role you have as a Key Person in forming very strong, positive relationships with parents or first carers.

Chapter 5: The effects of different cultures experienced by very young children

The response of the adult to the emotional needs of children remains virtually unchanged.

> Their bodies need moving, and their minds need discovering – of what is real, imagined and remembered. They want, not 'stimulation', but lively company that loves them and respects their eagerness to learn. Everything they know and do can be shared with affectionate partners. They cannot grow well, make friends or learn if they are tired, hungry, frightened, angry, bored or ashamed. These are constitutional givens of human beings from which all needs and social rights arise.
>
> (Trevarthen 2009 p. 1)

However, in the United Kingdom and world-wide, cultures are constantly changing because of the constraints placed upon Early Years Practitioners by government and because the related advice about best practice is changing all the time. An example of Government pressure is the Early Years Foundation Stage Framework that was implemented for all settings from September 2008. It was a very full document with supporting DVDs and information to enable Early Years Practitioners to respond to the needs of children and to extend their knowledge. The Framework included the Birth to Three Framework which had been well received and implemented by the Early Years workforce. The experiences of the children improved and the focus on play was welcomed, resulting in the improvement of play experiences in many settings. However, the impact of continuing pressure from Government has resulted in a gradual 'dumbing down' of the Framework. The result is a very slim, changed document that has gradually decreased in size through 2012, 2014, 2016 and 2017. The point about a curriculum reflecting the requirements of the Government was discussed by Nuttall (2003) in relation to changes in the New Zealand curriculum, Te Whariki. When first introduced the curriculum was seen to be vulnerable because,

> curriculum development is fundamentally a political act.
>
> (Nuttall 2003 p. 11)

A further point that is so pertinent to Early Years in the United Kingdom and related to not only this chapter but this whole book is that:

> early childhood education is a distinctive cultural form in its own right.
>
> (Nuttall 2003 p. 11)

How very true. As a final conclusion, you as Early Years Practitioners and Key Persons should remember this quote so that, when challenged about your practices relating to the emotional needs of children, you are able to articulate the reasons for them. You will be able to speak about the fact that their play and learning are child led. That you are offering play experiences that provide freedom for the children to choose and lead their play with an adult nearby to guide them. You will also be able to explain your ethos for working with parents and carers to ensure that each child's native language and culture are met. You are meeting their individual and emotional needs following communication with parents and carers and your own observations recorded in your setting.

Always remember, you have an immensely important role in the life of each of the key children with whom you work.

References

Barlow, J and Svanberg, P O (2010) *Keeping the Baby in Mind Infant Mental Health Practice*, Routledge: East Sussex

Blakemore, S J and Frith, U (2005) *The Learning Brain – lessons for education*, Oxford: Blackwell

Carter, R (2010) *Mapping the Mind*, London: Weidenfeld & Nicholson (Orion Books Ltd)

DCSF (2008) *The Statutory Framework for the Early Years Foundation Stage*, Nottingham: DCSF Publications

DfE (2012) *The Statutory Framework for the Early Years Foundation Stage*, Runcorn: DfE, accessed March 2014

DfE (2014) *The Statutory Framework for the Early Years Foundation Stage*, Runcorn: DfE, accessed March 2014

DfE (2016) *The Statutory Framework for the Early Years Foundation Stage*, Runcorn: DfE, accessed 23 February 2018

DfE (2017) *The Statutory Framework for the Early Years Foundation Stage*, Runcorn: DfE, accessed March 2017

Dowling, M (2010) *Young Children's Personal, Social and Emotional Development*, 3rd Ed, London: Paul Chapman

Elfer, P (2004) *The importance to infants of a keyperson who is well supervised and supported*, Research paper presented at Pen Green 3 July 2004.

Elfer, P; Goldschmied, E and Selleck, D (2003) *Key Persons in the Nursery*, London: David Fulton

Goldschmied, E and Jackson, S (1994/2004) *People Under Three* 2nd Ed, London: Routledge

Goouch, K and Powell, S (2013) *The Baby Room*, Berkshire: Oxford University Press

Gopnick, A; Meltzoff, A and Kuhl, P (2001) *How Babies Think*, London: Phoenix (Orion Books Ltd)

HMSO (2014) *The State of the Nation – Social Mobility and Child Poverty Commission* www.gov.uk/government accessed 23 February 2018

Holmes, J (2001) *The Search for the Secure Base*, East Sussex: Brunner-Routledge

House, R (ed.) (2011) *Too Much, Too Soon?* Gloucestershire: Hawthorn Press

Manning-Morton, J; Thorpe, M (2006) *Key Times – A Framework for Developing High Quality Provision for Children from Birth to Three*, Maidenhead: Open University Press

Moss, P (2014) *Transformative Change and Real Utopias in Early Childhood Education*, Oxon: Routledge

Nuttall, J (ed.) (2003) *Weaving Te Whariki*, New Zealand: New Zealand Council for Educational Research

Piaget, J (2002) *The Psychology of Intelligence*, Reprint, London: Routledge Classics

Shore, R (1997) *Rethinking the Brain: New Insights into Early Development*, New York: Families and Work Institute

Trevarthen, C (2002) Learning in Companionship in Education in the North: *The Journal of Scottish Education New Series*, No. 10, 2002 pp. 16–25

Trevarthen, C (July 2004) *Making Friends with Infants*, Paper presented at Pen Green Conference: Northampton

Trevarthen, C (2009) Why Attachment Matters in Sharing Meaning – HUMAN NEEDS & HUMAN SENSE: THE NATURAL SCIENCE OF MEANING, paper presented to the SAIA Seminar on Friday 11 September 2009, Glasgow file:///G:/Book%20-%20 Emotional%20Needs/Colwyn-Trevarthen-2009-Human-Needs-and-Human-Sense.pdf accessed 12 December 2017

Bibliography

Abbot, L and Langston, A (2005) *Birth to Three Matters*, Berkshire: Open University Press

Ainsworth, M, Blehar, M, Waters, E and Wall, S (1978) *Patterns of Attachment*. Hillsdale, NJ: Earlbaum

Arnold, C (2010) Understanding Schemas and Emotion in Early Childhood, London: Sage

Baker, C (2000) The Care and Education of Young Bilinguals: An Introduction for Professionals, Clevedon: Short Run Press Ltd

Barlow, J (2016) Improving Relationships in the Perinatal Period: What Works, in *AIMH UK Best Practice Guidance (BPG) No 1*, London: AIMH

Barlow, J and Svanberg, P O (2010) *Keeping the Baby in Mind Infant Mental Health Practice*, Routledge: East Sussex

Blair, C (2002) The On Track Guide – Section 1 https://www.beststart.org/OnTrack_English/pdf/OnTrack-Section1.pdf accessed December 2016

Blakemore, S J and Frith, U (2005) *The Learning Brain – lessons for education*, Oxford: Blackwell

Bligh, C; Chambers, S; Davison, C; Lloyd, I; Musgrave, J; O'Sullivan, J and Waltham, S (2013) *Well-being in the Early Years*, Northwich: Critical Publishing

Bowlby, J (1965) *Child Care and the Growth of Love*, 2nd Ed, London: Penguin

Bowlby, J (1969/1991) *Attachment and Loss: Volume1, Attachment* 2nd Ed, London: Penguin

Bowlby, J (1988/2005) *A Secure Base*, London: Routledge Classic

Bowlby, J (2005) The Making and Breaking of Affectional Bonds, Oxon: Routledge Classics

Bruce, T (Ed) (2012) *Early Childhood Practice – Froebel Today*, London: Sage Publications

Bruce, T and Spratt, J (2011) Essentials of Literacy from 0–7 – A Whole child approach to communication, language and literacy, 2nd Ed, London: Sage

Bruner, J (1996) *The Culture of Education*, USA: Harvard University Press

Bucci, W (1997) *Psychoanalysis and Cognitive Science: A multiple code theory*. NY: Guilford Press

Byron, T (2008) *The Byron Review* http://webarchive.nationalarchives.gov.uk/20100408 105219/http://www.dcsf.gov.uk/byronreview/ accessed 12 December 2017

Cameron, C; Moss, P and Owen, C (1999); *Men in the Nursery, Gender and Caring Work*, London: Paul Chapman Publishing

Carter, R (1998) *Mapping the Mind*, London: Weidenfeld & Nicholson (Orion Publishing Group Ltd)

Carter, R (2010) *Mapping the Mind*, London: Weidenfeld & Nicholson (Orion Books Ltd)

Child Poverty Act 2010 www.legislation.gov.uk/ukpga/2010/9/contents accessed 23 February 2018

Clarke, P (1996) Investigating Second Language Acquisition in Preschools. PhD thesis, Latrobe University. Published in Clarke (2009), in Bligh et al (2013) *Well-being in the Early Years* Northwich: Critical Publishing

Clyman, R B (1991) The Procedural Organization Of Emotions: A Contribution From Cognitive Science To The Psychoanalytic Theory Of Therapeutic Action in, *The Journal of the American Psychoanalytic Association*, pp. 349–382 https://www.scribd.com/document/172340247/Clyman-R-Procedural-Organization-of-Emotions-Affect-Psychoa-Perspectives-p-349-38219921 accessed 16 February 2018

Cole, M (1998) Culture in Development in *Cultural Worlds of Early Childhood*, Eds Faulkner, D; Littleton, K and Woodhead, M, London: Routledge

Comenius, J A (1628–1632) The Whole Art of Teaching, (http://www.froebelweb.org/web7005.html accessed 13 December 2017

Corel, J L (1975) *The postnatal development of the human cerebral cortex.* Cambridge, MA: Harvard University Press; http://www.urbanchildinstitute.org/why-0-3/baby-and-brain accessed on line 31 December 2016

Davison, C (2013) The Parents' and Extended Family Perspective in Bligh, C et al (2013) *Well-being in the early Years* Northwich: Critical Publishing

DCSF (2008) *The Byron Review – Children and New Technology*, Nottingham DCSF Publications

DCSF (2008) *The Statutory Framework for the Early Years Foundation Stage*, Nottingham: DCSF Publications

Deigh, J (1991) Freud's Later Theory of Civilization in *The Cambridge Companion to Freud*, Cambridge: Cambridge University Press

DfE (2012) The Statutory Framework for the Early Years Foundation Stage, Runcorn: DfE, accessed on line March 2014

DfE (2014) The Statutory Framework for the Early Years Foundation Stage, Runcorn: DfE, accessed on line March 2014

DfE (2016) *The Statutory Framework for the Early Years Foundation Stage*, Runcorn: DfE, accessed 23 February 2018

DfE (2017) The Statutory Framework for the Early Years Foundation Stage, Runcorn: DfE, accessed on line March 2017

DfES (2002) *Birth to Three Matters*, London: DfES Publications

DfES (2008) *The Early Years Foundation Stage*, London: DfES Publications

DoE (2011) Response to the Tickell Review of the Early Years Foundation Stage, London: DoE

DoE (2016) *An Early Years National Funding Formula*, UK: DofE accessed 11 October 2017

Donaldson, M (1978) *Children's Minds,* London: Fontana Press

Dowling, M (2010) Young Children's Personal, Social and Emotional Development, 3rd Ed, London: Paul Chapman

Elfer, P (2004) The importance to infants of a keyperson who is well supervised and supported, Research paper presented at Pen Green 3 July 2004.

Elfer, P (2008) *Facilitating intimacy in the care of children under three attending full time nursery*: unpublished doctoral dissertation. UK: University of East London. Findings were shared with delegates at the TACTYC Conference 2008

Elfer, P (2012) Emotion in nursery work: Work Discussion as a model of professional reflection in *Early Years an International Journal of Research and Development*, Volume 32, No 2, July 2012 Oxon: Routledge, Taylor and Francis Group

Elfer, P; Goldschmied, E and Selleck, D (2003) *Key Persons in the Nursery*, London: David Fulton

Fonagy, P (2003) The development of psychopathology from infancy to adulthood: the mysterious unfolding of disturbance in time', *Infant Mental Health Journal*, 24 (3): 212–239. May 2003 Accessed on line 10 April 2017

Garhart Mooney, C (2000) *Theories of Childhood*, St Paul, MN: Redleaf Press

Georgeson, J and Payler, J (2013) International Perspectives on Early Childhood Education and Care, Maidenhead: OU Press.

Gerhardt, S (2004) *Why Love Matters*, East Sussex: Brunner-Routledge

Goddard Blythe, S (2005) *The Well Balanced Child*, Gloucestershire: Hawthorn Press

Goldschmied, E and Jackson, S (2004) *People Under Three* 2nd Ed, London: Routledge

Goouch, K and Powell, S (2013) *The Baby Room*, Berkshire: Oxford University Press

Gopnick, A; Meltzoff, A and Kuhl, P (2001) *How Babies Think*, London: Phoenix (Orion Books Ltd)

Haralambos, M and Holborn, M (2000) *Sociology, Themes and Perspectives*, 5th Ed, London: Collins

Hay, S (1997) *Essential Nursery Management*, London: Bailliere and Tindall

HMSO (2013) Cross Party Manifesto – *The 1001 Critical Days*: HMSO

HMSO (2014) *The State of the Nation – Social Mobility and Child Poverty Commission* www.gov.uk/government accessed 23 February 2018

HMSO (2016) Cross Party Manifesto – *The 1001 Critical Days*: HMSO

Holmes, J (2001) *The Search for the Secure Base*, East Sussex: Brunner-Routledge

House, R (ed.) (2011) *Too Much, Too Soon?* Gloucestershire: Hawthorn Press

House of Commons Library – Funding for Maintained Nursery Schools 2017 UK:Gov accessed on line 11 October 2017

Jarrett, T and Perks, D (2017) *Funding for Maintained Nursery Schools* http://researchbriefings.parliament.uk/ResearchBriefing/Summary/CDP-2017-0033 accessed 1 March 2018

Johnson, T (2016) Holistic Development: The Social and Emotional Needs of Children, in *The Early Years Handbook for Students and Practitioners*, ed. Trodd, L, Oxon: Routledge

Liebschner, J (1992/2001) *A Child's Work, Freedom and Guidance in Froebel's Educational Theory and Practice* Cambridge: Lutterworth Press

Lumsden, E (2010) The New Early Years Professional in England

MacDougall, I and Brown, J (2016) The Foundation Years; Babies, in *The Early Years Handbook for Students and Practitioners*, Ed Trodd, L; Oxon: Routledge

MacNaughton, G (2005) Doing Foucault in Early Childhood Studies, Oxon: Routledge

Manning-Morton, J and Thorpe, M *Key Times - A Framework for Developing High Quality Provision for Children from Birth to Three*, Maidenhead: Open University Press

Marlen, D (March 2014) *A Gentle Beginning*, presented to the Royal Overseas League.

Marrone, M (2000) *Attachment and Interaction*, London: Jessica Kingsley Publications

McDowell Clark, R (2017) *Exploring the Contexts for Early Learning*, Abingdon: Routledge

Mooney, A and Munton, A G (1997) *Research and Policy in Early Childhood Services: Time for a New Agenda*. London: Institute of Education, University of London

Morris, K (2015) *Promoting Positive Behaviour in the Early Years*, Maidenhead: Open University Press

Moss, P (2014) Transformative Change and Real Utopias in Early Childhood Education, Oxon: Routledge

Nelson-Coffey, S K; Borelli, J and River, L M (2017) Attachment avoidance, but not anxiety, minimizes the joys of caregiving in *Attachment and Human Development Journal* 19, (5) pp. 504–531, Oxon: Routledge

NHS (2016) *Mindfulness* www.nhs.uk accessed 1 March 2018

Nolan, M (2016) 'The 21st Century Two Year Old: Ancient and Modern'. Presentation given at the SEFDEY National Meeting, March 2016

Nutbrown, C (2012*) Foundations for Quality, The Independent Review of Early Education and Childcare Qualifications,* London: DfE

Nuttall, J (ed.) (2003) *Weaving Te Whariki,* New Zealand: New Zealand Council for Educational Research

OECD/CERI (2007) *Understanding the Brain: the Birth of a Learning Science,* Paris: CERI - accessed on line 23 December 2016

Ofsted Report (2017) Bold beginnings: The Reception curriculum in a sample of good and outstanding primary schools London: Ofsted Gov.uk accessed on-line 13 December 2017

Pace, U; Zappulla, C and Di Maggio, R (2016) The mediating role of perceived peer support in the relation between quality of attachment and internalising problems in adolescence: a longitudinal perspective in *Attachment & Human Development* 2016 Vol. 18, No. 5 pp. 508–525, UK: Routledge

Page, J (2011a) Do mothers want professional carers to love their babies? In *Journal of Early Childhood Research 9 (3)* pp. 310–323 London: Sage

Page, J (2011b) *Professional Love in Early Years Settings: A Report of the Summary of Findings* https://www.bing.com/search?q=Jools+Page+Professional+Love+2011&src=IE SearchBox&FORM=IESR4S&pc=EUPP_UE02 accessed 27 February 2018

Paley, V G (1999) *The Kindness of Children,* USA: Harvard University Press

Paley, V G (2001) *Mrs Tully's Room, A Childcare Portrait,* London: Harvard University Press

Pally, R (2000) *The Mind-Brain Relationship,* London: Karnac Books

Palmer, S (2006) *Toxic Childhood,* London: Orion Books

Pascal, C and Bertram, T (1997) *Effective Early Learning,* London: Hodder and Stoughton

Piaget, J (2002) *The Psychology of Intelligence*, Reprint, London: Routledge Classics

Piaget, J and Inhelder, B (1969) *The Psychology of the Child,* USA: Basic Books Inc

Pinker, S (1995) *The Language Instinct*, Penguin: London: The Penguin Group

Praglin, L (2006) The Nature of the "In-Between" in D.W. Winnicott's Concept of Transitional Space and in Martin Buber's das Zwischenmenschliche in *Universitas Vol 2 Issue 2*

Public Health England (2015) Guidance Childhood obesity: applying All Our Health, Gov.UK

Quan-McGimpsey, S; Kuczynski, L and Brophy, K (2011) Early education teachers' conceptualizations and strategies for managing closeness in child care: The personal domain in *Journal of Early Childhood Research* 9: 232 originally published online 21 April 2011 ECR: Sage, accessed on line 13 December 2017

Read, J (1992) A short History of Children's Building Blocks in *Exploring Learning Young Children and Blockplay,* ed. Gura, P; London: Paul Chapman Publishing

Reber, A S (1995) *The Penguin Dictionary of Psychology*, London: Penguin

Reid, S (1999) Developments in Infant Observations, The Tavistock Model, London: Routledge

Roberts, R (2010) *Self-Esteem and Early Learning,* London: Sage

Rose, J; Gilbert, L and Richards, V (2016) *Health and Wellbeing in Early Childhood*, London: Sage

Rousseau, J J (1762) *Emile*, trans. Foxley, B, Great Britain: Amazon

Rutter, M and Rutter, M (1993) *Developing Minds,* London: Penguin The New Early Years

Sadler, J E (undated) *Comenius* https://www.britannica.com/biography/John-Amos-Comenius) accessed 3 November 2017

Science Media Centre (2011) *expert reaction to the biological effects of day care as published in The Biologist, a journal of the Society of Biology* www.sciencemediacentre.org/expert-reaction-to-the-biological-effects-of-day-care-as-published-in-the-biologist-a-journal-of-the-society-of-biology-2-2/ accessed 27 April 2014

Scott, K (2017) Response to the Ofsted report on Bold Beginnings, in *Nursery World* (8 December 2017), accessed on-line 13 December 2017

Shore, R (1997) Rethinking the Brain: New Insights into Early Development, New York: Families and Work Institute

Shore, R (2001) 'Effects of a secure attachment relationship on right brain development, affect regulation and infant mental health', *Infant Mental Health Journal*, 22 (1–2), pp. 7–66

Siegal, D (2012) The Developing Mind: How Relationships and the Brain Interact to Shape Who We Are. New York: The Guilford Press.

Sigman, A (2011) Mother Superior? The Biological Effects of Day Care, *The Biologist. 58, pp. 29–32*

Siraj-Blatchford, I (2010) Diversity, Inclusion and Learning in the Early Years in *Contemporary Issues in the Early Years;* 5th Ed, eds Duffy, B and Pugh, G; London: Sage

Solly, K (2015) Risk, Challenge and Adventure in the Early Years, Oxon: Routledge

Standards and Testing Agency (2016) *Early Years Foundation Stage Profile Handbook* https://www.gov.uk/government/uploads/system/uploads/attachment_data/file/564249/2017_EYFSP_handbook_v1.1.pdf accessed 1 March 2018

Steele, H (2002) State of the Art Attachment The Changing Family, *The Psychologist* Vol 15, No 10, UK BPS/Wiley pp. 518–522

Stern, D N (1998) *The Interpersonal World of the Infant,* London: Karnac Books

Tabors, P (1997) One Child, Two Languages, in Bligh et al (2013) *Well-being in the Early Years* Northwich: Critical Publishing

TACTYC (2017) *A Response to Ofsted's (2017) report, Bold beginnings: The Reception curriculum in a sample of good and outstanding primary schools* by TACTYC (Association for Professional Development in Early Years). December 2017 accessed 13 December 2017

Taggart, G (2011) Don't we care? The ethics and emotional labour of early years professionalism in *Early Years, An International Journal of Research and Development*, Volume 31, 1 pp. 85–95

Tardos, A (2010) Introducing the Piklerian developmental approach: History and principles pp. 1–4: *The Signal*, International Association for Infant Mental Health Jul–Dec 2010 USA www.waimh.org/files accessed 20 September 2017

The Concise Oxford Dictionary (1995); 9th Ed, ed. Thompson, D; Oxford: Oxford University Press

Thomas, E (2017) Exploring residential mobility: Learning about how young children experience the transition of moving-house and how adults can best support them, Presented at the TACTYC Conference, Birmingham, November 2017

Thomas, N (2001) Listening to Children. in *Children in Society*, eds Foley, P; Roche, J; Tucker, S, Hampshire: (Palgrave Macmillan) Open University Press

Tovey, H (2008) Playing Outdoors Spaces and Places Risk and Challenge Maidenhead: OU Press

Tovey, H (2013) Bringing the Froebel Approach to your Early Years Practice, Oxon: Routledge

Trevarthen, C (1998) The Child's Need to Learn a Culture in *Cultural Worlds of Early Childhood*, eds Faulkner, D; Littleton, K and Woodhead, M, London: Routledge

Trevarthen, C (2002) Learning in Companionship in Education in the North: *The Journal of Scottish Education New Series*, No. 10, 2002 pp. 16–25

Trevarthen, C (2003) *Chuffedness – the Motor of Learning*, Pen Green Conference, June 2003

Trevarthen, C (July 2004) *Making Friends with Infants*, Paper presented at Pen Green Conference: Northampton.

Trevarthen, C (November 2005) Conference Presentation at Pen Green: Northampton.

Trevarthen, C (2009) Why Attachment Matters in *Sharing Meaning HUMAN NEEDS & HUMAN SENSE: THE NATURAL SCIENCE OF MEANING* file:///G:/Book%20-%20 Emotional%20Needs/Colwyn-Trevarthen-2009-Human-Needs-and-Human-Sense.pdf accessed online March 2017

Trevarthen, C (2011) What young children give to their learning, making education work to sustain a community and its culture in 'European Early Childhood Education Research Journal, The Journal of the European Early Childhood Education Research Association, Oxon: Routledge, Taylor Francis Group, pp. 173–193.

UK Welfare Reform Act 2012 www.legislation.gov.uk/ukpga/2012/5/contents/enacted accessed 23 February 2018

Ward, U (2016) The Child Family and Society: Working in Partnership with Parents, in *The Early Years Handbook for Students and Practitioners*, ed. Trodd, L; Oxon: Routledge

Whalley, M (2001) *Involving Parents in their Children's Learning*, London: Paul Chapman Publishing Ltd

Whinnett, J (2012) Gifts and Occupations: Froebel's Gifts (Wooden Block Play) and Occupations (Construction and Workshop Experiences) Today, in *Early Childhood Practice – Froebel Today*, ed. Tina Bruce, London: Sage

Winnicott, D W (1971) *Playing and Reality*, (2005 Ed Routledge Classics) Oxon: Routledge C

Winnicott, D W (1977) *The Piggle*, London: Penguin

Woodhead (1998) The Cultural Worlds of Early Childhood, London: Routledge

Websites

file:///C:/ INetCache/IE/H9I0XYFR/Summary_State_of_the_Nation_2014.pdf accessed 14 October 2016

http://1.bp.blogspot.com/-xqrpQjqQiX8/T4GJukJ6grI/AAAAAAAABVU/mOeQ_6YVKNk/ s1600/instinctual+brain.gif accessed 21 December 2016

http://myjc.jc.edu/users//holley/LittleBoy.htm accessed on-line 19 September 2017

http://www.1001criticaldays.co.uk/news-press-releases/1001-critical-days-conception- age-two accessed 8 December 2017

http://www.childdevelopmentmedia.com/articles/mary-ainsworth-and-attachment-theory/ accessed 5 March 2017

http://www.froebelweb.org/web7005.html accessed 13 December 2017

http://www.learningdiscoveries.org/StagesofBrainDevelopment.html accessed 21 December 2016 Originated in Prentice Hall. Diagram of brain

http://www.multilingualliving.com/2010/05/31/does-bilingualism-multilingualism-cause- language-delay/ accessed 11 December 2017

http://www.robertsonfilms.info/young_children_in_brief_separation.htm

http://www.who.int/about/mission/en/ accessed 31 December 2016

https://www.heritagedaily.com/2013/10/roman-skulls-discovered-under-liverpool-street-station/99123 accessed 23 November 2017

www.aimh.org.uk

www.beginbeforebirth.org/for-schools/films#womb accessed 7 January 2017

www.education.gov.uk/publications

www.healthline.com>health>placenta accessed 12 January 2017

www.legislation.gov.uk/

www.midwifery.org.uk accessed 12 January 2017

www.nhs.uk/Conditions/stress-anxiety-depression/Pages/mindfulness.aspx accessed December 2017

www.northumberlandlsgb.proceduresonline.com accessed 12 January 2017

www.sciencemediacentre.org/expert-reaction-to-the-biological-effects-of-day-care-as-published-in-the-biologist-a-journal-of-the-society-of-biology-2-

www.uni.edu/universitas/archive/fall06/pdf/art_praglin.pdf

www.webarchives.gov.uk

www.who.int/about.definition/en/print.html

Index